CHRIST'S TWELVE

(Henoch).. non apparuit: quia   tulit eum Deus. Genes. 5. 24.

F.M.S.

Ecce currus igneus et equi   ignei diviserunt.. IV. Reg. 2, 11.

CHRIST'S TWELVE

REV. F. J. MUELLER

ST. AUGUSTINE ACADEMY PRESS
HOMER GLEN, ILLINOIS

Nihil obstat: H. B. Ries, Censor librorum
Imprimatur: ✠ Samuel A. Stritch, Archiepiscopus Milwaukiensis
October 1, 1931

This book was originally published in 1931
by The Bruce Publishing Company.

This facsimile edition reprinted in 2019
by St. Augustine Academy Press.

Chart in appendix taken from
Visualized Church History by Sister Mary Loyola Vath

Public Domain Illustrations have been added.

ISBN: 978-1-64051-097-5

Fratribus sororibusque,
Amicissimis mihi semper.

For permission to reprint these sketches, the author's thanks are due to the Editor of *The Sign*, in which publication they first appeared substantially as they are now.

INTRODUCTION

THE Apostles of Christ are interesting people; scarcely any men in history have been equally so. Of a truth, "the proper study of mankind is man"; and when it is a question of the men that Christ associated with Himself in His public career, and made His legates after His earthly life was done, what little we can know of them is well worth the effort and time it entails to know it. It does cost plenty of both. It is part of the alluring interest of these twelve men that we know so very little about them at first hand. Contemporary records have very little to say about them. Their immediate successors had other and seemingly more important things to do than to write down for us what manner of men it was that Christ chose for His Apostles. Pagan historians of their day and the day that followed immediately after them, knew them only as so many strange and alien figures preaching an alien creed with strange and rather offensive vehemence, rather than as individuals.

And yet there can be no manner of doubt at all that they were individual, strikingly so. We think of them often, too often, probably, as a group, as if they had no separate and individual characters at all. Nothing could

be further from the facts in the case, for even the little
bits and stray scraps of information that have come to
us across the years leave no room for doubt. They were
men, strong men after their own fashion, and in God's
own good time, eminently successful men. History
knows no group of men that more signally succeeded
in an enterprise of prime weight and worth. If only
because of the impress they have left on mankind and
its subsequent record on earth, they deserve to be
known as well as the circumstances of the case permit.

That is none too well, certainly; we know distressingly little about them and scarcely anything directly
from them. Here and there, scattered incidentally
through the Scripture narratives of their Lord and
Master, you may happen upon a few meager though
suggestive facts about their characters. But for the
most part, of them as of other strong men who were
too busy doing things and getting things done to write
about how they were done, we must, in this day and
age, nineteen centuries after the event, deduce what
they were, mostly from what they did and from the
manner in which they did it. After all, there are worse
indexes to a man's character than his deeds. And for-
tunately, something of what the Apostles did and the
way they did it, we do know, and at first hand.

So, these character pictures must not appear under
any false colors. They do not, and they cannot in
reason, pretend to be anything like final or complete
and certainly accurate pictures of the men they undertake to portray. They are, when all is said and done,

no more than one man's interpretation of the few and scanty facts we have on good authority about Christ's Twelve. *Ex pede Herculen,* is a motto that has a goodly antiquity to recommend it, even if not much else. It is the process by which these sketches perforce had to grow, if they were to grow at all. Tiny little facts; occasional speeches; praises from their Master or, oftener, rebukes; consternation or indignation upon occasion; ignorance or weakness or downright stupidity or treachery in action — these are the stray bones that had to serve to build up their likenesses. They could not be induced in any sense to sit for their portraits; they were too busy for that. It remains only for us to pierce beneath the surface of the Gospel story of their deeds and their association with the Master of that first Seminary for Souls, as well and as completely as reason and the Faith and the due exercise of what may be termed historical imagination may permit.

For into these portraits have gone several ingredients. The Gospel story, along with the accounts given in the Acts of Apostles, has been, and of course by necessity, the prime source of information concerning the men who are written about directly nowhere else in contemporary document. Traditions about them and their work and their labors and their deaths cluster in masses, of course; it would be strange if, after the lapse of so many centuries of men thinking more or less about them, that were not the case. But few of such traditions are at all reliable, and not in the case of any of them may one be certain that they have not been added to or lessened in their course across the ages. But sometimes they do serve to throw light into some dark corners of apostolic history, and by doing so they serve us well. Then there is the thing I have called historical imagination, the faculty or quality that enables us of the twentieth century to throw ourselves, partially and imperfectly it is true, into the scenes and circumstances in which the Apostles lived and loved and labored. There is an evident danger in the use of that faculty; we are entirely too prone to read into the case what we know and feel, after this lapse of time, and to misinterpret thereby. Still, there can be no historical writing of any sort without it. It is to be hoped it has not been in any instance permitted to overstep its legitimate bounds to present any Apostle in a false light.

There remains only to say a word as to the purpose of these sketches. It is not to present any new discovery; that is obvious enough. It is not to present any of the Apostles in a new light. It is, primarily, just to make the Apostles human beings. We are, all of us, entirely too much given to the mistake of regarding the saints in general as marvels of grace, so far beyond the ordinary human channels as to be made of another clay. That, of course, is miles from the truth. The basic truth in any saint is his human nature, and the Apostles, all of them, are delightfully and fundamentally human. No marvels of grace they, from childhood to the grave. No born saints they, without human temptations and human passions and human failings; but entirely human things, made of the same sort of fallible clay as the rest of us. The presentation, then, of those strikingly different human characters by which the Apostles were what they were; the picture of their strengths and their weaknesses; the play of lights and shadows in their characters — that is the prime purpose of this little book. If it should succeed in promoting appreciation of the labor of the Apostles, and in inspiring thereby devotion to them, now that they have proved themselves glorious heroes through grace and their intense devotion to their Divine Master, so much the better. And if, further, the spectacle of these very weak and fallible human beings who became, through their love for Christ, the marvels of grace and strength they certainly were, should inspire some one soul to rise superior to his painfully human shortcomings and strive onward and upward toward the light, I shall be more than content.

F. J. M.

CONTENTS

1

CHRIST'S TWELVE

IT IS a tribute to the radical impress of Christian history on mankind, that no man reading the above title is even for a moment at a loss to interpret it. Who should Christ's Twelve be, if not the dozen individuals we have agreed to call Apostles? They are those chosen ones from among the comparative handful of Christ's converts during His earthly life to whom He gave a special character and mission. They are, in a unique sense, His chosen, for though He had come to call all men to salvation and to redeem all mankind through His Passion, still, there was a specially designated group of men who were privileged to hear His especial invitation to leave all and follow after Him, even though it meant in the long run a special participation in Calvary. "Come, follow Me," He said to one after another of these, and their number is twelve.

Chosen in different circumstances, chosen at different times during the three years of our Lord's public life, sharply individual and divergent in characteristics one from all the others, they yet agree in this, that they heard the invitation and call of Christ and did just what He asked of them, mighty sacrifice though it was for all of them: "Leaving everything, they followed Him." They agreed, too, in this, that they were honored and benefited with about three years of close, personal friendship and intimacy with the most sublime Personality that can ever tread earth. Well did our Lord say to them on one occasion: "I no longer call you servants, but friends." What a title of nobility was thus conferred, and for all eternity. The Friends of Christ *par excellence!* That character of the Twelve is enough in itself to arouse our interest in their personalities.

What sort of men were these that Christ so signally honored with His friendly intercourse and invited to accompany or follow Him even to Calvary? About to die, He said to them, "Go forth, preach the Gospel to every creature; as the Father hath sent Me, so I send you; and behold, I am with you all days even to the end of time." A glorious commission and a wonderful promise for their continued support and comfort in the trials their mission would inevitably entail! It cannot be a matter of indifference to us who have benefited by that mission what manner of men it was to whom these weighty words were spoken.

They were not chosen, to begin with, from Christ's previous friends. It may even be true of the apostolic band, counting therein along with the original Twelve the added Paul and the Judas-substitute, Matthias, that none of them had ever seen Christ before the day of election. Several of them, tradition says five of them, were distantly related to our Lord; namely, the two James's, John, Jude, and Simon, but none of them had been intimates of His in any sense before the day when they heard that thrilling and compelling invitation to leave everything and follow Him in His life and His death. They were all natives of His native land, however, as it was quite natural, humanly speaking, that they should be. For the first appeal of the God-man was to be made to His own, to the Chosen People of God; theirs was to be the first chance to accept or reject the words of salvation. So it was Jews that Christ chose for His Apostles.

They were hard-working men, every one of them, nearly all of them what we might be inclined to designate now as "outdoor men." Not one of them was of the effeminate stripe; a saintly priest is authority for the assertion that not even God could make a saint of a mollycoddle! Most of them worked with their hands, and painfully hard, obeying literally the injunction of Eden to Adam: "In the sweat of thy brow shalt thou eat bread." Some of them were fishermen, rough, uncouth, crude in manners probably, strong-willed, strong-passioned, independent in spirit. One of them, Matthew, was a publican; Judas was perhaps a steward; Philip was a fellow townsman of Peter and Andrew but not a fisherman apparently; Paul was a soldier and scholar. But all of them, it would appear, were of the hard-working type of man; and appropriately, for the task they were to be given after the Ascension of Christ was no child's play, but a task for manly men.

Education seems not to have been very conspicuous among them. It is entirely probable that some of them could not even read and write. It is debatable whether there was in the ranks of the Apostolic Fourteen anything like a college education of these days with the exception of Paul and possibly Bartholomew. In one word, all that is certainly known of their antecedents and their early characters justifies the conclusions that they constitute in general a commentary on the assertion that "the weak hast Thou chosen to confound the strong." For judged by every available human standard, as compared with the task of evangelization that they were assigned, they were emphatically of the earth's weaklings.

And how that fact must have told in the common Gentile appreciation and estimate of them and their mission after they dispersed to carry out the injunction to preach the Gospel to every creature. Among the Jews, their human characteristics might conceivably have been arguments for their mission; in the Gentile world, they could have been nothing short of almost insuperable handicaps. Imagine the situation; set in the Rome of the Caesars. It was a luxurious world, that Roman world. It was built on human pride; the patrician of Rome thought himself the best and finest thing in existence. He worshiped after a fashion the thousand and one gods that had made Rome great, as he considered. His morals were of his own making; pleasure was the god he actually worshiped by that day, leaving aside all that early, strong paganism, that had made his forefathers clean and healthy-minded to a high degree. Force was right; revenge was a duty — if it did not entail too much exertion; hatred was a matter of course after an injury or an assumed slight, and forgiveness an effeminate weakness. His days were spent in the luxury of the baths and his nights in riotous banqueting. Rome had once been a city of brick; he saw it a city of marble, a great and splendid thing in the eye of the sun. One day, this Roman princeling, this favorite of a thousand gods, happens, in the Forum, on a short, stumpy, gnarled-handed, straggly-haired Jewish fisherman who proceeds to tell him and all his ilk that their lives are all wrong; that forgiveness is a dictate of the One True God; that they must forever abandon their life of luxurious ease and substitute a life of penance and mortification; that their despised slaves are at least as worthy as themselves and in many cases a great deal better; and that, finally, they must abandon all the pantheon of Roman and Greek and imported gods and goddesses and worship the One True God, the Christ, a crucified Jewish criminal. It was to laugh, of course, at first hearing. And the preacher of that outlandish doctrine? Only a Jew, and an ignorant Jew at that. And the haughty patrician drives on the slave bearers of his sedan chair and there is a new joke in the warm-room of the bath that afternoon. And nothing more, for the time, nothing until the Roman saw thousands of men and women and children die in torment rather than forswear that fantastic new religion of the Jew fisherman who preached a crucified Christ.

Some such impression must the first announcement of Christian doctrine have made through the personalities of its preachers all around the Gentile world of the first and second centuries. The original preachers of Christianity were all Jews, to begin with, and the world of that day hated Jews just as thoroughly as they are hated and despised generally now, if not more so. The Apostles were all Galileans, except St. Paul and Judas, so that even the rest of the Jews hated and condemned them. "Can any good come out of Nazareth?" was a sneer that more than one Jew must have echoed. They were ignorant men, for the most part, untrained and uncultured, ignorant of the amenities of life and social intercourse, not eloquent when eloquence is judged by ordinary standards — once again, with the exception of St. Paul, who is one of the world's great orators. They were renowned for nothing in the world of culture and intellect, except St. Paul once more, for he was know to the Roman world, and well known, for his consummate ability. The weak things, truly, had Christ chosen to confound the strong, and the Graeco-Roman world of the day was strong in its entrenched position. And yet, these ignorant Twelve, plus the genius Paul, blasted the Graeco-Roman world from its position and preached Christ Crucified with so good effect that within 50 years, not only was the Christian dogma preached and believed and treasured all over the known world, but the very emperor of Rome, the embodiment of the Roman state religion, regarded as a sort of incarnation of the divinity of the Roman gods, was himself a follower of the lowly Nazarene. A wonderful triumph, beyond any doubt.

It is more than a wonderful achievement; it is humanly speaking, an impossible one. It is a first dictate of logic that there be a proportion between cause and effect; the qualities of the effect cannot be more than those of the cause that produced it. The achievement of the Apostles, on this first principle of common sense, proves their mission divine. For there can be no questioning the effect produced; it was no less than the conversion of a pagan world to Christianity. The means, humanly speaking, are ridiculously inadequate. No twelve men, not the best twelve men in creation, much less twelve ignorant Jew fishermen, could have produced that stupendous result. And yet the result was produced. The conclusion? Simple enough; the Twelve were not the causality behind the effect but only the instruments of that causality.

Some idea of the inadequacy of the Apostles as the cause of the world's conversion to Christian truth may be gleaned from a distant comparison. What chance, think you, would there be to convert, not the whole world, but Pittsburgh, to some one change of mind, let us say, in its politics? What chance is there that the twelve best and finest men on earth could make Pittsburgh predominantly Socialist in politics? Endow those apostles of Socialist principles with all the eloquence you will, give them all the chance possible, compel the populace to listen to the presentation of their case, give them all the time there is — can it be done? Hardly. And yet, it was not one city the Apostles converted, but a goodly portion of the world, and not to a change of political allegiance, but to an abandonment of everything that was deep seated and fundamental in the Gentile consciousness, and that, despite all the obstacles their own personalities inevitably threw in the way of success in their preaching. No, there is no escaping the conclusion; the Apostles were successful because it was the power of the Holy Spirit that spoke in them and through them. They were themselves but instruments in the hands of a divine power, and divinity there is no withstanding. But what instruments they were! They appear across the ages to us in their corporate capacity; we speak of them constantly as the Twelve Apostles, unconsciously aligning Paul with them, but they were men strong in their own individuality. There is no monotony about them; they were thirteen live men, human beings essentially, with their faults and foibles as well as noble strengths, made up of very ordinary flesh and blood, real men ennobled through the friendship of Christ whom they preached and for whom they lived and died.

Not that Christ found them capable and adequate instruments for His purpose at once, as soon as they were enlisted in His band; they were still sometimes painfully, exasperatingly human beings. They were destined for a divine mission; they remained long earthbound. Their thought was long in purely terrestrial terms. They were to help establish Christ's kingdom on earth and failed totally to appreciate or realize that it was a heavenly kingdom that should be on earth among men, made up of men, governed by men, and yet not essentially either human or earthly. For three years their Great Master instructed them in the enormous significance of His Kingdom on earth, and yet, at the Last Supper, there was more than one speech from several of the company that proves their thought on the matter was still earth-clinging. A three-year course in the divine seminary had not been enough to purge the earthiness and the mental inertia from these Twelve. But with all their faults — and they had and retained more than a few to the Day of Pentecost — they were likable, lovable men, all the more so, from our viewpoint, because they were not impossible paragons of perfection and virtue, but flesh-and-blood human beings, made up of good and bad qualities, compounded of strength and weaknesses, just as are the rest of mankind. They are not puppets, but men. They became heroes — all but that one abysmal failure — through a flaming personal devotion to an ideal, the ideal of God made man for man's lasting good.

2

PETER, The Man of Impulse

THERE is no more delightfully human figure among the Apostles of Christ than their prince. He is a strong man, a hearty lover of Christ, a real fighter upon occasion, impetuous and impulsive to a fault sometimes, delightfully human in his strength and his weakness, for he had both the admirable and the faulty qualifications of the impulsive temperament. From the first day when his brother Andrew came to him and told him that he had seen the Messias, he is the man of noble simplicity; he allows himself to be taken at once to the Master, and is received by Him with a special welcome, a welcome that is not paralleled in the case of any other of the chosen friends of Christ. For we are told in the simplicity of the Gospel style, that "Christ looked upon him and said: Thou art Simon, the son of Jona, thou shalt be called Cephas which is interpreted Peter." On the spot, the alliance is sealed forever between the Saviour and the essentially human being whom He had destined to be His first vicar upon earth.

There is no other human character in the Gospels

that we know so well and so completely as the soul of Peter, for from that first meeting with his Master, Peter had but one ambition and one aim in life, to be with the Master he loved so wholeheartedly. It is almost safe to say that wherever Christ had any company from among His Apostles for the last three years of His earthly life, Peter was at His side. And how our Saviour must have loved that man of hearty impulses, loved him even in his faults, which were not few or trivial — wherein Peter is like most people of impetuous disposition. It is idle to debate, as it has been long and acridly debated, whether it is Peter or John the Beloved whom Christ loved most tenderly. That Peter had a special place in the heart of Christ is obvious to anyone who reads the Gospel account of their companionship and the elevation of the erstwhile fisherman to the headship of the Apostles. From their first meeting, Peter's manly spirit attached itself to his Lord in a special fashion, and none of the Apostles seem seriously to have questioned at any time Peter's supremacy among them, even before Christ had officially inducted him into office as head of the apostolic company.

Peter was born Simon, the son of Jona, a resident of Bethsaida on Lake Genesareth. Andrew was his brother and Philip came from the same town, though apparently he did not share the occupation of the others in the lake waters. Of his early life, there is almost nothing known for certain, save tradition tells that he was married and living in Capharnaum at the time of Christ's public mission. He seems to have been success-

ful in a moderate degree, for he owned his own boat.
On the other hand, he and Andrew worked their boat
alone, whereas the boat of Zebedee, their fellow townsman and associate in the fisheries, had his two sons,
James and John, as well as several hired sailors, for
crew. Tradition, likewise, is authority for the statement
that Peter's wife had died before his call to the apostolate, and that he was living with his mother-in-law
when Christ called him to be a fisher of men. He
seems to have been a trifle younger than Christ, consequently a man about thirty or scarcely that, when
they met on the Jordan whither Andrew had conducted him to meet the Master. It is a mistake, therefore, to conceive of Peter at the time of Christ's early
life as a man in advanced years. He was, on the contrary, a man in full vigor and health, a man of vigorous
action and ardent disposition, a man of action rather
than of painstaking thought, the sort of man, consequently, that all great active enterprises must needs
enlist to get difficult work done.

He had been attracted, as had many of his fellow
citizens of the lake district, to the teachings and the
austere life of the Baptist, and had been among those
to whom John had announced the Lamb of God who
taketh away the sins of the world. He had joined
Christ, thereafter, and accompanied Him, notably to
the wedding feast at Cana, and then had gone back to
his home and his trade on the lake till he received
along with Andrew his final and definite call to the
apostolate. It happened on that great day when the

miraculous draught of fishes after an unfruitful night's toil had shown Peter and Andrew as well as the others there that their Master was more than man. "Henceforth ye shall be fishers of men" was the prophecy spoken by Incarnate Wisdom, and "leaving their nets and all things, they followed Him."

As for his physical appearance, there is no authentic portrait that has come down to us across the centuries. Tradition of the most ancient sort, however, shows him as of medium height, well proportioned, broad shouldered, hardened by toil. His hands were a workman's hands, gnarled and calloused, and on occasion torn and bleeding, through his work at the oars and the nets. His complexion is said to have been normally pale, but the exposure must have tanned his skin considerably. His eyes were dark with the fire of the impetuous man in them, with the crow's-feet at the corners that the glare of the sun on water naturally produces. His hair in early manhood was thick and crisp, his beard dark and curly, his features somewhat heavy, with the strong mouth and the rather square jaw of the man of action and strength of character. Toward the end of his life, however, his eyes had lost much of their glint because of the tears he shed over his sad treachery to his Friend and Master, his hair had thinned and grown gray, his step had lost some of the youthful spring of earlier days, but to the end he was a man to withstand physical effort, essentially a man to get things done. But though the years left the marks of their passing on his frame; though his face was furrowed with the track of the tears, as tradition says it was; mentally and spiritually, temperamentally, he remained the Peter who was always first to speak and first to act. His impulsiveness of spirit remained to the day of his death.

It is, perhaps, his most conspicuous characteristic; he was never anything if not impetuous. He was the sort of man who would speak or act, and then think it over afterward, often enough in deep regret. There was in him both the strength and the weakness of that character of man. He could never have been accused of deliberate malice in any of his mistakes and failures, for he seems almost never to have been deliberate in anything he did or said. In him there was no guile, no craft, no shadow of deceit possible. He wore his heart on his sleeve; his sentiment constantly ran away with his judgment, or, at least, ran on before it. Whenever he spoke, he spoke what he thought, and fearlessly, and his action was just as impetuously brave, save on one momentous occasion that he was to regret all his days. This impetuous activity breaks out again and again. When Christ, for example, had spoken to the multitude on the lake shore about the Blessed Sacrament and they had left Him because they found it a hard saying, He asked His Apostles if they too would leave Him. It is, as always, Peter who breaks out into speech. "Lord," he says, "to whom shall we go? Thou hast the words of eternal life." When Christ foretells that all the sheep will be scattered and the shepherds with them, that that same night all the Apostles will leave Him, it is Peter who proclaims so confidently that though all the others should leave their Master, he will not betray his Lord. When Judas and his mob invade the garden to apprehend the Christ whom they feared to take in the city in daylight, it is Peter who draws his sword and defends the person of Christ against the hideous treason, only to be sharply rebuked for his pains. But how Christ must have loved the great heart of the man while rebuking his lack of judgment! Again, when our Lord foretells to the Apostles His coming passion and death, Peter exclaims eagerly: "Lord, be it far from Thee; this shall not be unto Thee." And once again he is sharply rebuked: "Go after Me, Satan, thou art a scandal unto Me, because thou dost not relish the things that are of God but the things that are of men." When the Apostles see Christ from their boat, the rest of them seem to have been content to look and say, awe-stricken, "It is the Lord." Peter throws himself from the boat and swims to meet Him. And so the Gospel story goes on, nearly every page of it telling some incident wherein Peter takes the lead, where he is the impulsive, tempestuous character that makes him so invariably attractive despite all his mistakes, because the fault is always so obviously not of the heart but of the head. Even when he is a blunderer he is an entirely lovable blunderer whose warm heart and ardent love for Christ are his excuse.

He is not in any sense void of humility, however, in his leading. That, too, stands out of the man's character like a lighthouse on a rocky shore. He may be first,

perhaps alone, in loudly proclaiming his entire devotion to Christ though all others should faint and fail
Him; he is likewise first and most conspicuous in his
regret and repentance for any fault. In the boat, after
the miraculous draught of fishes, he falls on his knees
at the feet of Christ to exclaim: "Depart from me, O
Lord, for I am a sinful man," not deeming himself
worthy to be in the same boat with his Master. When
Christ, the great night before His Passion, would wash
His Apostles' feet, it is Peter who exclaims that the
thing shall not be, but when he is emphatically told
that unless Christ wash his feet he shall have no share
in eternal life, he would be washed not only in feet,
but hands and head as well.

His selection by Christ as head of the Apostles gave
him no sense of inflation, no exaggerated notion of his
worth. He remains completely humble in word and
action, as his writings and the writings of his disciples
show. He knows his authority, to be sure; he is in no
way proud and haughty in his exercise of it, always
willing to admit his mistake if he be shown to have
made one. When Paul, for instance, a new Apostle, a
reformed persecutor of the Church, dares to withstand
Peter to his face in a dispute over a point of discipline,
Peter admits his own error and rectifies his faulty
policy. His humility of spirit leads him to impel his
disciple Mark to tell, in words that he must have
known and meant to be everlasting, the detailed story
of his treason to Christ. The other Evangelists tell as
little of the sad story as possible; in the Gospel accord-

ing to St. Mark, written by the chosen friend and disciple of Peter for the instruction of the Roman Christians, the tale is told in full detail, sparing Peter not a whit in the telling. A noble public penance, beyond all disputing, for the great mistake of a great man's life, the one saddest blemish on a life's devotion to a great love.

For Peter's devotion to Christ, in personal friendship and loving reverence, is the mainspring of his whole life after his call to the apostolate. It is the explanation of all his words and all his hasty deeds; he is the embodiment of personal love for Christ, a whole-souled, manly love and devotion to a friend and leader. It is Peter who exclaims in words that ring with exultant sincerity: "Thou art Christ, the Son of the living God." It is he who cries out in accents of intense love: "Master, Thou knowest that I love Thee." It is he who promises to follow his Lord to the death and eventually keeps that promise though the way led through the bitter valley of sin and repentance. For repent of his denial of Christ he certainly did.

What a scene is that, the scene of the denial of Christ by His chosen Apostle, one of the most stirringly dramatic scenes of the whole awful drama of the Passion! Christ had been dragged through the streets at night, chained like a malefactor, and Peter and John had followed Him afar off in sorrow, far enough behind to avoid arrest and near enough to keep His sacred Person in sight. They enter the court and mingle with the soldiers about the fire, for it is a Palestinian night and chilly then. A servant girl sees Peter and speaks to him, "Thou art His follower?" There is nothing strange in the question, or alarming either, for he was known well enough as a friend of Christ's, and moreover, witnesses for the defense were guaranteed immunity. And yet Peter denies his friendship for Christ. Once again the charge is made, and yet again, and proved by Peter's Galilean accent; and now Peter, thoroughly enraged, and perhaps more than a little alarmed, denies with an oath that he knows his Lord. "I know not the Man," he cries. And just then, Christ is led through the court, and denier and Denied are face to face. The oath-bound blasphemy falters and dies on the Apostle's lips; his Lord speaks to him not a word, but casts just one look of reproachful disappointment upon him and is dragged away to judgment and to torture. And Peter? What of Peter? He is filled with sudden remorse and sorrow; he has forsworn the love of his Friend and Master, and he rushes out to speak no more with his Lord before the tragedy is consummated on Calvary. He rushes out into the night, alone with his grief and regret; goes forth to a lifetime of penitence, weeping bitterly in his sorrow. And his tears, and better, the contrition and love of which they are the external expression, save him from the fate of that other Apostle who sinned no more deeply but repented not at all save in despair.

A true man, then, this chief of the Apostles, a man with faults and failings entirely human; a man irresolute upon occasion and yet with the strength of imperishable granite he clings with the greatest fidelity and love to Christ, and then alienates himself from his Beloved after years of devotion by one hasty action, regretted ever after. He is rash and reckless in word and action, hasty in all he does and says; he is full of zeal and enthusiasm, insists he will not desert his Master though all others desert, and he it is precisely who does so first and foremost. He dashes into the melee with a sword in Christ's defense and that same night himself falls victim to human respect and fear of ridicule. He loves with a manly love, and denies his love at the challenge of a servant girl. But as he has been first in sin, he is first, too, in sorrow; his contrition, like everything else he does, is from his inmost soul. He loves his Lord too much to despair as Judas does; his reliance on Christ's mercy overpowers his shame and remorse; the agony of his soul rushes to his Saviour through his eyes in one glance of perfect repentance and love, and he goes forth to do his Master's bidding, to continue his Master's work, and govern his Master's loved ones in His name, till he puts the seal on a lifetime of service and love by dying on a cross, the sport of a mob for Christ, crucified, at his own humble request that rejects too close a likeness to Christ, head downward. A noble man, truly, and a lovable one!

3

JAMES, Son of Thunder

WHEN Jesus went to the house of Jairus to cure
his daughter, He took with Him Peter and
James and John. On the day of the Transfiguration,
that wonderful day when Christ for an instant allowed
His divinity to shine through and illume His human-
ity, it was Peter and James and John who were permitted to witness the wonder. When His hour was at
hand, and His soul was sorrowful even unto death,
the night before His Passion, as He went into the
garden to pray, in His desire for a touch of human
sympathy, He took with Him once more the same trio
of friends, Peter and James and John. In short, in the
most momentous events of His life, when there was
any human companionship whatever, it was always
these same three special friends that Christ chose to
bear Him company. And that unfailing human quality, curiosity, perforce wonders why it should always
have been the same three. For Peter, the reason is not
far to seek; he was the destined vessel of election as
Christ's vicar on earth after the Ascension. In the case
of John, the traditional position he held as Christ's

specially beloved virgin disciple explains his presence at Christ's side when only two others were chosen from among the Twelve — occasions, it is worth noticing, when His Mother herself was absent. But why always James? What sort of man can James the Greater have been that he should be so privileged along with the two others whose personalities are so much more vivid to us through the narratives of the Evangelists? For it is a strange thing that there is so little told in the Gospels about this man who stood so close to the side and heart of his Master. But the little we know positively of him makes him a strikingly appealing personality, a lovable man.

He was a native of Bethsaida, the son of Zebedee and Salome. Through his mother, he was rather closely related to the Saviour Himself, for Salome was either the niece or cousin of the Blessed Mother. Of Zebedee we know no more than the name, unless there be truth in the tradition that says he became one of the disciples of Christ. Of Salome, we have a bit more of information; she was one of the "holy women" who followed after Christ on His preaching tours. She was, therefore, probably present, too, on Calvary when He was crucified, and was one of the first to see the Risen Lord on Easter Day. Tradition continues her history and puts her in the rudderless boat to which the Jews committed Martha, Mary Magdalene, and Lazarus, and several others, and which the winds drove to the shores of France. James was the eldest son of Zebedee and Salome, born about the same year as Christ, two years before his brother John. It is possible that the brothers were acquainted with the Child Christ; perhaps that, along with their relationship, serves to explain their early adherence to Him and their acceptance of His mission as the Messias when they first learned of it.

Any description of James's physical appearance could be no more than guesswork. But he seems to have been a man of at least ordinary education and cultural training, with plenty of opportunity to come in contact with the Greek life that was in his day rather generously spread along the shores of his native lake. At any rate, Galilean as he was, everything about his early life predisposed him to accept the claims of the Messias when He made them public. True, he did not at once recognize Christ as God; none of the Apostles did that. True, likewise, is it that he looked forward with the rest of the Twelve to the expulsion of the detested Romans and re-establishment of the splendid kingdom of David and Solomon. It was not till comparatively late in Christ's life that any of His Apostles rose to the idea of a spiritual kingdom that should be in this world but not of the earth, earthly. Still, James had been one of the most ardent disciples of John the Baptist, and when that hero of God pointed out Christ on the Jordan, saying: "Behold the Lamb of God," James followed his brother John to the Messias, and began his life of devotion and love. With the other Apostles chosen by then, they accompanied Christ to Cana for the wedding feast and returned thereafter temporarily to their nets, to leave them and everything else earthly

to follow Christ in His apostolate when He gave them
the definitive summons to be fishers of men.

But little that James said in the course of the years
he spent in his novitiate with Christ has come down
to us. He was a man of few words, apparently, thinking, while the more impulsive Peter broke into speech.
He was one of the strong, silent men that do so much
of the world's great work and get little credit in the
shape of popular acclaim for so doing. Self-effacing he
was, save on one memorable occasion, and very probably that occasion is in no way to his discredit. A
plain, blunt man, no orator, ardent none the less in temperament, outspoken when he spoke at all, he merits
the name Christ gave him when he was called a "son
of thunder" by the flaming, bounding love and affection of his manly soul for the best friend he knew, his
Lord and Master. He was constantly at Christ's side to
assist when assistance was possible, to save from annoy-
ance when that could be, to console in hours of stress
and anxiety, not with words but by his silent, manly
sympathy. Can it be that it was for that wordless sympathy of the man that Christ chose him for one of the
three who should watch an hour with Him in the
dread night of His humiliation?

There are several occasions, however, when he broke
into speech, and on all he was rebuked by his Divine
Friend, albeit gently and lovingly. In one instance, the
inhabitants of En-Gannim refused a night's hospitality
to Christ and His Apostles. Incensed and indignant,
James and John cried out: "Lord, wilt Thou that we

command fire to come down from heaven and con-
sume them?" And turning He rebuked them, saying:
"You know not of what spirit you are. The Son of
Man came not to destroy souls but to save." It was a
not unnatural outburst of pained indignation toward
inhospitable people that called forth this declaration of
Christ's essential purpose on earth, and surely He was
not hard to move to forgiveness of His beloved Sons
of Thunder. It shows the Sons of Thunder in some of
their essential characteristics, with a clarity that words
can do little more than obscure. It reveals much of
their characters. They were indignant at the hardness
of the townspeople who could thus flagrantly close
their doors in the very face of the Master who had not
whereon to lay His head and would accept hospitality
at their hands. The great brothers broke out, at the
sight of that hardness of heart, into stormy and mistaken speech that betokens their great love for Christ
just as much as their mistaken notions of His manner
of action. They burn for action; they long for retribu-
tion on the inhospitable citizens of the little city; they
would have incivility punished in a fiery rain. And for
their pains, they hear Christ's gentle rebuke.

Another occasion suggests itself, the famous incident
when James and John, first through their mother and
then personally, asked of Christ seats at His right hand
and at His left when He should come into His Kingdom. It looks at first sight like a display of ambition
or vanity, as if the Thunderers were avid for high position in the earthly kingdom they expected Christ to

establish. So, often enough, has it been interpreted. But
there is another interpretation that fits the facts as well,
taking their request not as the expression of ambition,
but as a demonstration of the purest and noblest friendship for Christ. His hour, He had said, was approaching; He was going up to Jerusalem to give Himself
over to His enemies. The trial was at hand, and what
more natural than that the impetuous ardor and love
of the Thunderers should dictate that they strive to
associate themselves more and more closely with their
Master in His day of difficulty? Their request was dictated by tenderness and courage. And as such Christ
met it. "You know not what you ask," He said. "Can
you drink of the chalice that I drink of, or be baptized
with the baptism wherewith I am baptized?" There
is involved here a magnificent testimony to friendship,
human friendship for Christ. James knew the meaning
of the question, well enough; he realized it meant sacrifice and renunciation, pain and defeat, a share of the
world's hatred, for these were the bitter chalice and the
freezing baptism that Christ foresaw for Himself and
the friends who would choose His fate as their own.
With a lovable smile, therefore, can we conceive Him
saying to the two heroes: "You shall drink of the
chalice that I drink of; and with the baptism wherewith I am baptized, you shall be baptized; but to sit
on My right hand or on My left, is not Mine to give
you, but to them for whom it is prepared." It was not
selfish ambition, then, that prompted that request for
the place of honor in Christ's kingdom; James had

counted the cost, knew that the place of prominence and honor was likewise inevitably the place of greatest danger, and it was there that his love for Christ and his courage in the face of the danger that threatened Christ bade him be. And later, after his Master had left the earth so much poorer by leaving it, the same James did fulfill Christ's prophecy: he did drink of the chalice that Christ had meant, and drained it to its bitterest. For he was the first of the Twelve to shed his blood for Christ.

He was present in Jerusalem during the early persecution at the hands of the Jews. He was a shining light among the early Christians in Jerusalem. It is no undue stretch of imagination to see him among the spectators when Stephen was stoned as he prayed for those who stoned him. Can it have failed to enter deep into that thinking soul of James, that spectacle of sacrifice and of love for Christ? Ten years later, Herod embarked on a career of persecution to consolidate his political position. He and his satellites hated the sect of the Nazarene, and knew James as one of the pillars of the Early Church. Their plans would be so much more easy to attain if James were out of the way! With its tragic baldness, the Book of Acts of Apostles tells the story tersely: "Herod, the king, killed James, the brother of John, with the sword." No more than that; no heroics about it in Luke's account of the martyrdom of James in Jerusalem. How it all accords with the antecedents of the story. "Can you drink of My chalice?" asks Christ. "I can," says James. "Herod, the king, killed James, the brother of John, with the sword." Words can hold no more of pith or meaning than these.

His last act of life was of a piece with all the rest, if tradition may be credited. The tale has it that he had been apprehended by the minions of Herod through the betrayal of a certain Josias. But the miscreant was so impressed with the quiet courage and steadfastness of James that he himself believed and professed his belief openly. James baptized him just before his own martyrdom, and the Thunderer appeared before the judgment seat of the Redeemer whose chalice he had just drunk, in company with the soul of his erstwhile enemy and accuser. It was a fitting climax to a career of quiet, strong love and service. It required an ardent courage to face the destiny that Christ's words revealed to James; he had it to the full, love-inspired as it was, and the event proved that it was no idle boast that he made, in company with his great brother, when he boldly proclaimed his readiness to drink Christ's chalice with Him or after Him. True, like the rest of the Apostles, he failed once. When that chalice was first offered his lips, he recoiled from it. He fled on the dread night of Judas's treachery, like the rest of them. The remainder of his life, however, redeemed that one blemish, that one act of faulty courage in which even Peter and John shared. Like any other of the followers of Christ to the death, he attracted to himself the hatred and enmity of entrenched greed and selfishness, and he must die that Herod's political plans might not miscarry. He died as he had lived, intimately beloved by Christ, inspired with purest manly affection for his Friend, living out a love that won for him through its resistless ardor the title of Thunderer.

4

JOHN, The Beloved

THE originator of the conventional artistic represen-
tation of St. John has much to answer for. It is the
commonest thing in the world to see the Beloved Disciple of Christ presented as a mild, gentle weakling, of
the effeminate species of mankind. And certainly there
can be no greater nonsense than that. Who, seeing one
of these stained-glass notions of St. John, would ever
suspect spontaneously that it is intended to represent
one of those whom Christ Himself called Sons of
Thunder? What is there in the figure of an effeminate,
soft youth to justify any such vigorous characterization
as is essential in that name of Thunderer? There could
be no greater mistake, certainly, for whatever else John
may have been or not been, weakling he unquestionably was not. There is simply nothing weak or effeminate in his make-up at all, and to represent the man as
a fop or mollycoddle is totally to miss the salient point
of his character.

That point is strength of soul, for it requires a strong
man to arouse that affectionate regard that Christ and,
after Christ, Mary and Peter especially, had for the

Beloved Disciple. So far from accurate is that weak notion of John, that his early career as an Apostle gives the impression rather of impetuous, headlong vigor in action. He shows himself a man of temper, vehement, indignant temper. He was a fisherman, to begin with, like his brother James and the other set of brothers whom Christ called first to the Apostolate, Peter and Andrew; and to earn one's living with boat and net in the open lake could have been no child's play. That took manhood, and John had manhood to a nobly high degree. In the absence of any and every shred of evidence, we could justifiably conclude to the strong quality of the manly character of John; did not Christ love him? And not even the tenderness and affection that were his major role in the drama of the redemption can properly obscure the strength of soul, the nobility of character, that made that love possible. No weakling, then, was John, but a thorough, complete, noble man, truly a Son of Thunder.

If there were no other evidence of it, the scene when Salome asked Christ for the two places of honor at His side for her two sons, James and John, proves the high quality of John's manly character. The two heard their mother's request and repeated it eagerly. Not vulgar ambition or mere lust for power and distinction dictated that strange request. They knew well enough that Christ was about to go into extreme danger, and the place of honor could not fail to be as well the place of highest danger. Their friendship for their Master was such, however, that precisely there they would be;

hence the great request, and the noble answer it obtained from Christ: "Ye know not what ye ask; can you drink of the chalice of which I shall drink? And can you be baptized with the baptism wherewith I shall be baptized?" In other words, "Can you find it in you to bring the sacrifices and bear the brunt of the position you ask?" Immediately, eagerly, hotly, comes the answer: "We can." And with a kindly smile that must have been a benediction on those on whom it fell, Christ promises, not the places at His right hand and His left in His eternal kingdom, for those, He says, are not His to give them but must be given to those predestined therefor, but a special share in His love and friendship; they should drink of His chalice, and right royally was that promise kept in afterdays. It was no weakling, but a real, manly man that spoke that eager assent: "We can," and it was no weakling that could have fulfilled the divine promise of drinking of Christ's own bitter chalice as John was to drink.

There was nothing effeminate in another scene between Christ and His Apostle, the scene, namely, when the little town turned them away inhospitably and John would call down fire from heaven to punish the inhabitants. Son of Thunder, Christ then called him, and led His band away elsewhere to obtain the night's shelter here denied them all; but it could not have been entirely sternly that He regarded the affection of the Apostle that spoke the hot request for permission to punish. A rebuke it did extort from Christ, it is true, for the fiery zeal that would so avenge the affront. Not yet was John the man of brotherly love for everything human that he was to become later under the mellowing influence of his memories and Christ's graces. Son of Thunder he showed himself that evening, and surely Christ must have been touched at the zeal and love that spoke themselves so eagerly in His defense, even though it did not accord with His plans to permit so signal a vengeance for the insult. A vigorous, outspoken, frank, honest, manly man was John, therefore; impetuous and fiery to a fault, unrestrained then, but strong with a virility and fire that required only the touch and transformation of grace to temper into complete charity that should remake the man.

There is no trace of special predilection for John before the Last Supper, unless, indeed, it be the promise of Christ's chalice to the two Sons of Thunder, and that took place just a few days before the Passion. Nowhere does the expression "the beloved disciple" or the "disciple whom Jesus loved" occur in the Gospels till that last great night of Christ's earthly life. The eager outcry "We can" spoken by James and John claimed places of special friendship for Christ and the claim was tenderly allowed. John's position as Christ's specially beloved was evidenced at the Last Supper. Our Lord had spoken touchingly of His impending doom. He had thrown into the midst of the sorrowing Apostles the bombshell of the treachery that one of them was about to perpetrate. They whispered among themselves as to the identity of the culprit. John did his whispering to better purpose. He asks his Master, in

all the simplicity of a noble and trusting affection, and
his question obtains the answer that points out Judas
as the traitor. And when the betrayer departs in con-
fusion to consummate his treachery, John accompanies
Christ to the Garden as one of His chosen three to
watch through the dread night that was to witness
the first act of Calvary's drama. When the false friend
betrays Christ with a kiss, the true friend is there by
His side, and it is probable that he left all vigorous
defense of Christ to the impetuous Peter, not because
of his fear, but because he better realized that no such
defense did Christ require. His love for Christ and his
devotion to His interests were no less than Peter's certainly; his judgment was better on that occasion. The
Son of Thunder had been schooled a little more in the
school of love and had learned the lesson that Christ
impressed then on His intrepid defender, that He
could have called on legions of angels for His defense
if defense had been His purpose or desire. John, by that
time at least, had learned the love-inspired lesson of
Christ's divinity. His love would not permit him to
remain long away from Christ. True, he did flee, like
the rest of the Apostles, in fright when the mob
dragged their Master through the dark streets of Jerusalem to judgment and to death. But he regained his
wits immediately and, with Peter, followed the sad
progress of Christ to the court of the guard. He did
not remain long away; his love for Christ and his ap-
prehensions would not have permitted that in any
case. He returned to the courtyard, and the return

bespeaks his flaming courage as much as anything ever could. From the persecutors of Christ he had fled, and cravenly; into their very midst he returns as soon as possible. His courage matches Peter's, for both loved enough the Master whom they had a little while before deserted, to return into what must have seemed to them the very jaws of danger, the court of the guard itself. How long he there remained is matter for no more than conjecture; one wonders, for instance, if he accompanied Peter when the Prince of the Apostles had perpetrated his treason and rushed away into the night in penitence for his sin. Or did he rather feel the more impelled to remain behind, just exactly because Peter had gone, that there might be at least one of Christ's friends near Him that dreadful night of woe and terror? The Gospel record is silent on the matter; but we do find John, the Beloved, where love could expect to be found, beneath the Cross on Calvary. Both his courage and his love drew him there, and not all the danger to be apprehended at the hands of those from whom John had once fled could deter him then. His head might well pay the price, the head that had rested on Christ's bosom during the Last Supper; no matter. Love makes its demands, and John's was a noble and manly love. Chivalry, too, called upon him; Mary was there, in the midst of that mob milling about the foot of the Cross, and Mary must be protected, cost what it might. So, Christ's dying glance rested upon Mary and John together, mother and son henceforth.

There John's faith and trusting love were tried in

the fiery furnace of apparent defeat. Christ had proclaimed Himself Messias, God. John saw Him die in
disgrace and utter overthrow. His love proved stronger
than all possible doubts, and the agony of his soul must
have shone forth through the eyes of the man as he
gazed upward into the glazing eyes that he so tenderly
loved. What Christ read there would require Christ
Himself to tell. Some of it, we may deduce from the
remarkable thing that Christ did there. "Son, behold
thy mother; mother, behold thy son," He said from
His gibbet to those two whom He loved so greatly,
His own mother and His cousin-disciple, John the
virgin. He would complete His sacrifice and die bereft
of every and any consolation on earth; He gave His
last legacy to John, and through John, to us, when He
resigned Mary to John's care for the rest of her earthly
sojourn. It was an enormous proof of Christ's love for
John, certainly, and Mary's too, for we are told, simply
and nobly, that from that day, John took her into his
charge, her friend and her protector, till the day when
her noble heart attained its desire and her love freed
her soul from the trammels of flesh and allowed it to
mount exultantly to reunion with her Son and God.
Truly, the promise of Christ to John was kept. He did
drink of Christ's chalice there on Calvary and the place
of special friendship that he claimed for himself was
given him in far greater measure than he could have
hoped or suspected.

A great proof of the quality of exalted manhood to
be found in all the Apostolic College is their entire

freedom from petty jealousy. The preferences of Christ for Peter and James and John, if evidenced to men of inferior quality, would have caused fierce antipathies inspired by jealousy of the favored ones. In the ranks of Christ's Twelve, there is nothing of that sort; they had learned their lesson in too fine a school, under too great and inspiring a Master; there was no room in those great, manly souls for anything so pitifully small and mean as jealousy of those of their number who stood in a closer relation to their Master than the rest. And the Gospel story gives reason for the belief that after the Ascension of Christ, under the presidency of Peter consequently, the intimate association between Peter and John continued unbroken. James was the first of the Twelve to die. Peter and John were associated in their ministry to an exceptional degree. There is obvious a special affection between them, with more than a tinge of respect of John for his chief. They were associated in their flight from Gethsemani and in their sorrowful pursuit of Christ into the very court of His enemies. They were foremost in rushing to the sepulcher on that first glorious Easter, and there John, the speedier of the two, gave a delightful proof of his respect and affection for Peter, as well as that quality of considerateness that we, for want of better word, call tact. John was first at the tomb; he awaited Peter's arrival, so that the Chief of the Apostles might be the first to have the ocular proof of the Resurrection on which they were to base what is still the most convincing proof of the divinity of their Master. Later, Peter

and John were together when they went to the Temple
and Peter healed the man who begged for alms at the
Gate called Beautiful. They were together when ar-
raigned before the Sanhedrin, and together they were
sent by the Apostolic Body to Samaria to lay hands on
the neophytes of the deacon Philip there. Neither
Christ nor Peter conferred on John any specially great
powers of the Ministry, no powers greater than those
of Jude or Philip or Thomas, for example. But both
found in John a friend and companion to trust and
to love, and Mary nobly seconded both in that affection.

The years that John spent in the intimate company
of the Blessed Virgin after the Ascension were forma-
tive years, surely, even though he had been great of
soul by the time of Calvary's tragedy. What soul would
not grow — a veritable clod, certainly — when privileged with the daily conversation and companionship
of the Mother of God? It was from her that John obtained some of the information of the earlier years of
Christ's career on earth that formed the subject of
much of his meditation, and the association on so intimate terms with the Blessed Mother could not fail to
mellow and purify and strengthen and elevate that
great soul whom Christ had so signally favored with
guardianship over the greatest and noblest of God's
creatures. Small wonder, certainly, that the burden of
John's preaching in the last years of his life should
have been invariably love. When, old and infirm,
already a martyr for Christ though miraculously
snatched from the cauldron of burning oil in which

tyranny and hatred of Christ had plunged him, he looked with his eagle-sighted vision to the very majesty of the Trinity Itself, it was Love and again Love and only Love that he preached to those who gathered about his venerable form to listen to the message of the last of the Apostles.

A noble figure he certainly was in the evening of his long life. "My little children, love one another. It is the commandment of the Lord, and if you will keep it, it will be sufficient." Nobly true! "By this shall all men know that you are My disciples, if you have love one for another." So Christ had laid down the test; what else could John teach, when he would present the very heart and soul of the message of Christ to mankind, than this: "My children, love one another; that is enough!" And with that message of deathless love on his aged lips, still young in spirit — for was he not the disciple whom Jesus loved? — though he had seen all the rest of that noble band precede him into the company of their Master through the martyr's gate, death overtook him in the early years of the second century. In the city of Ephesus his sorrowing disciples buried him, but his spirit is deathless. His message of love still thrills the souls of countless Christians and the Gospel he wrote to vindicate the divinity of his Lord against impious heretical attack, stands as not only a matchless literary achievement, but as a proof, love-inspired, that Christ is more than man, on the testimony of one who lived with Him and loved Him deathlessly.

John is an immortal, beyond all doubt, in the hearts
of men, for he is one of the most lovable characters in
history. Impulsive and fiery enough to merit the title
of Thunderer, he was made of noble stuff, and when
it had been tried in the crucible of love, he emerged as
nearly worthy of the Apostolate of Christ and the
guardianship of His Mother as flesh and blood can be.
He was virginal, even though some tradition sees in
him the bridegroom of the wedding at Cana. It is no
wonder that he was deemed most worthy to pillow
his troubled head on the great heart of Christ at the
Last Supper, and thereafter to be son and guardian of
Mary in Christ's own stead. As an Apostle, he was, in
the words of another of that noble company, "solici-
tous for all the Churches," and sealed the compact of
love with Christ with the sacrifice of his life. He
earned the palm of martyrdom though saved from
martyr's death, and in his subsequent exile at Patmos,
was privileged to pierce into the future of the Church
on earth and in heaven with prophetic vision that still
remains, after the march of nineteen centuries, the
mysterious Apocalypse. He was content to spend the
last years of his life quietly, resting from his labors,
communing in the sanctity of his great soul with the
Master whose call could not then be long in coming;
it was not to be. The honor of Christ and the dignity
of His Mother were impiously challenged, and John
became once more the penman of God. Pouring out
the love of his soul, he wrote that fourth Gospel that
deserves to be called the Gospel of the Heart, the

Gospel of Love, wrote it with an unsurpassable sweep and mastery that is sublime and convincing from its noble prologue, "In the beginning was the Word and the Word was with God and the Word was God," to the explicit conclusion that repeats the keynote of it all: "These are written that you may believe that Jesus is the Christ the Son of God, and that believing, you may have life in His name." It is a fitting conclusion to a life's work that began in tempestuous zeal and closed in a zeal, less impulsive, but just as noble, for what greater thing could come from the mind and heart of the Disciple whom Jesus loved than the Gospel of Christ's love for men?

5

ANDREW, Another Man's Brother

IT IS a noteworthy fact that the first four of the Apostles of Christ to be called to leave everything mundane for the divine Apostolate were two sets of brothers. Peter and Andrew were brothers, and so were James and John. And throughout the earthly life of Christ, these four seem to constitute, as it were, an inner circle among the Twelve, as if there were admitted among them some pre-eminence in favor of the men whom Christ called first. It would seem that the earthly reputation of Andrew has suffered to some extent what very much resembles eclipse. He occupies the rather unfortunate position of being another man's brother. The very first time he is mentioned by name in the Gospels, it is in that capacity. "Andrew, Simon Peter's brother" — that is the title he bears on that first occasion. And it would appear that so far as the record speaks specifically, Peter's brother he remained to the end of his life. Not that he was not an individualized personality; he is individual enough wherever he is mentioned at all. But the fact remains that very little of his action and only a sentence or two of his speech have come across the years to enlighten us about his personal characteristics, as a man's words and actions invariably reveal his personality to all who know him. A man can no more hide his personality in the record of his deliberate speech and his action than the sun can hide his face; actions speak, proverbially, and they tell the story of personality better than volumes of talk. A man may perhaps camouflage his real self in his public talk; not every man who addresses an audience is careful to reveal all himself. But in a man's actions you may read him to the full, and the bits of this obscure Apostle's work that have been preserved for us either in the Gospels or in a genuinely reliable tradition show him a man of strong character and immediate decision. Of his speech we have almost nothing; of his action, specifically very little, aside from what we know he must have been and done as a member of that body of Christ's friends who accompanied Him almost constantly for the last three years of His life. But that little is significant.

He was a resident of Bethsaida, by the Lake of Genesareth, younger, it would appear, than his famous brother, Simon Peter. Like Peter, he was a fisherman, his brother's partner in the boat that Christ honored by using it for a pulpit on a great occasion. He seems to have been living in the same house with Peter when the revelation of the Messias came to his notice. He was evidently a man of some little education at least, a man of thought as well as of daily toil with his hands, the sort of man that appears to have been attracted most generally to the preaching of the Baptist. For Andrew was one of the followers of that great and austere preacher of penance. He was present that day on the bank of the Jordan when John, enlightened from on high, saw approaching him the figure of the new Preacher and Teacher in Israel. No hesitation in the Baptist; there never was! "Behold the Lamb of God," he cries, and with an immense joy that his mission has been accomplished, he salutes the Messias he has been announcing. Precursor he had been by God's ordinance, herald of mankind's coming redemption. The last of the prophets, it was reserved for him to see with his own eyes the Redeemer whom forty centuries of prophecy had foretold to the Chosen of God. John saw Him and hailed Him in His proper character at once. "Behold the Lamb of God."

In that exclamation, heaven-dictated as it unquestionably was, there was light for more than John. Andrew at once perceived the meaning of it, saw through the veils that had hitherto concealed the person of the Messias, and recognized in the approaching Christ the personality of the Expected of Centuries. His decision is made at once; the matter admits of no delay. He follows the Messias at once, and we are told that Jesus, seeing that He was followed, asked: "What seek you?" And he is bidden, "Come and see." So it was done; Andrew and his unnamed companion went with Christ, saw where He dwelt, and remained with Him that day. And returning home, he betakes himself at once to his brother and says, with no shadow of hesitation whatever: "We have found the Messias." And at once, Andrew takes Peter to the Master who greets him with those momentously prophetic words: "Thou art Simon, the son of Jona: thou shalt be called Cephas which is interpreted Peter." So Andrew, though not himself the leader of the Apostles nor the greatest personality among them, has the distinction of being the first of the Apostles to hear the call and answer it, and likewise, the further distinction of bringing to Christ the man of destiny, Peter, His vicar on earth.

It is proof of his generosity and consideration for others, that he did not keep his great news to himself. It would have been inconceivably selfish to do so, and in Andrew there was no room for selfishness. He had found what centuries of the Jewish people had longed for; the Messias had been revealed to him in a flash. Who knows how long Andrew had been himself on the search, in his own quiet, unobtrusive fashion? Manifestly, the time of the Messias was close at hand; the prophecies of generations were being rapidly fulfilled. Andrew's master, John the Baptist, had been preaching the Redeemer's close advent. It is in no sense surprising, therefore, that Andrew was not startled when the dramatic indication was finally given there on the banks of the Jordan. He heard and saw and followed after Christ. He was entirely convinced that the Messias stood before him in human shape, spoke in human speech, though the shape and the speech were not so patently royal as Andrew with all the rest of his generation had been misled into expecting. But once confronted with the flaming personality of Christ, there is no hesitancy about Andrew; his decision is made on the spot, and without any attempt at dramatics, he bursts into his home where Peter is and announces in all simplicity, as great things are simple always: "We have found the Messias." The news had to be shared, and who so close to Andrew then as his great brother? Immediately, side by side, the two hurry out along the road once more, till Peter sees the Master for himself, and Andrew rejoices in Peter's joy at the finding of the Messias. Great-souled and generous as he is, Andrew's heart expands with shared joy, for what pure joy is not the greater for being shared?

On one other occasion in the Gospel narrative does Andrew play a speaking part. It is the great day when the thousands had followed Christ into waste places without food for the journey, and the sympathy of Christ was touched at their predicament. He could not send them away fasting for they would faint on the way, and where were they to find food in the wilderness for so many? Andrew finds the answer. He sees near by a lad with a lunch basket. "There is a boy here," he says, "with five loaves and a few fishes." But, he adds deprecatingly, "What are these among so many?" Is it entirely illegitimate exercise of fancy to suspect that Andrew may have had some inkling of the great event of the next hour? May we not reasonably suppose that after he had seen some of the other wonders that his Master had so considerately wrought for the alleviation of men's necessities, he was quite well aware that the case was not so hopeless as it looked? At all events, while the rest of the Apostles stood helplessly by, wondering what could be done, it was Andrew who saw the opportunity and seized it at once. It required a mighty confidence in Christ and His powers to suspect that in a boy's lunch there might be hidden potentialities of sustenance for thousands, but whether or not he suspected what Christ might do, it is quite certain that it was he that spoke up and called his Master's attention to the youth and his scanty store of food. The rest is history. The loaves and fishes were miraculously multiplied to satisfy five thousand appetites as a symbol of the satisfaction of millions of times five thousand spiritual appetites through the Bread that Christ came upon earth to bring. And it was Andrew of quick decision that saw the opportunity and brought the boy to Christ, as he had once brought his brother.

Again he filled his role of bringing men to Christ. A few days before the tragedy of Calvary, a group of Gentiles came up to Jerusalem, met Philip, and asked if they might see Christ. Philip, as though doubting the propriety of the introduction, refers the matter to Andrew, apparently as to one better equipped for the decision. Could the Master be disturbed for the sake of these Gentiles? Perhaps they came only out of vulgar curiosity anyhow. Andrew solves the riddle at once. He takes them to Christ, and the Master makes of the occasion an opportunity to address to all within earshot one of the most significant and moving discourses, as the twelfth chapter of the Gospel according to St. John records it. Notice, all three of the instances where Andrew is named in the Gospels are similar in this respect: all of them consisted, from his viewpoint, in bringing souls to Christ. And what marvels did not our Saviour do with them, once they had come in contact with His personality!

That same role was Andrew's during the years that followed the Ascension. With the others, he had been commissioned to preach the Gospel to every creature. With the rest, after their friendly farewells in Jerusalem after Pentecost, he took his staff and went into the great world to preach Christ and Him crucified. Whither his missionary journeyings took him, there is no certain knowledge and no tradition that is entirely unexceptionable. The most probable accounts have him preaching the Gospel manfully in Cappadocia, Galatia, Thrace, Macedonia, Byzantium (the modern Constantinople), and Achaia. It is generally believed that he was put to death during the reign of Nero, on November 30, A.D. 60. The traditions concerning his death are well known. The form of cross on which he suffered bears his name, and the holy joy with which he greeted his gibbet is proverbial. All his life long, from the first acquaintance with his Divine Lord to the end, from about the year 30 to the year 60, Andrew had done one thing and done it supremely well; he had lived for the one purpose of serving Christ and his fellow men by bringing men's souls to know Christ.

The closing scene of his life was of a piece with the
rest of it. From his gibbet, during his long agony —
and he was bound on the cross to protract his suffer-
ings — he preached to those who came about that
agonized deathbed, and the burden of his preaching
can have been no other than the Christ whom he had
so long loved and served. What matter to him that the
Gospel calls him "brother of Simon Peter." Honor
enough for him it was that Christ had called him
friend and treated him so, and it was to his Great
Friend that the angel of death, reversing Andrew's
lifelong role, would bring him rejoicing.

6

PHILIP, The Prosaic

NO CHARACTER study of the Apostles can fail to note the outstanding fact that they were so different one from another in character and temperament. "In My Father's house there are many mansions," says Christ, and in His own chosen body of immediate personal friends there are all sorts and conditions of men; they range from men of action, like Peter, and poets, like John, to matter-of-fact people, like Philip. There is little, really, that is certainly known of Philip beyond the few facts that the Gospels record of him. We know, however, that he was an inhabitant of Bethsaida, the lake town that furnished so surprisingly great a portion of the membership in the College of the Twelve. It was from that little place that Christ called Peter and Andrew and James and John; Philip was also of that place, but what his mode of life was before his call to the apostolate, the records do not tell. He was apparently not a fisherman as the rest of the Bethsaida Apostles were; but more than that it would be mere conjecture to say, and one guess is as good as another. Of his antecedents we know just as little. It is known, however, that he was a member of the crowd on that momentous day, so great in its significance to Christian history, when John the Baptist pointed out the Messias and in so doing, concluded his mission upon earth. It was to announce and point out immediately, and not in prophecy as his predecessors had done, the personality of the Messias. His preaching and the sensation it created in the neighborhood were intended for that purpose; it was done when he saw the figure of Christ nearing him there on the banks of the Jordan that day and cried out in exultant joy: "Behold the Lamb of God who taketh away the sins of the world." More than one of those who later became Apostles of Christ were among those who heard that cry of fulfilled hope and longing, and Philip was among them. His apostolic life, his career of bringing souls to Christ, began on the spot.

It is interesting to note how often that means was used by Christ in becoming humanly acquainted with the persons of His Apostles. One member of a pair was used to bring the other, more than once, often enough in fact to suggest the possibility that there is hidden deep in that fact some significance that has escaped scrutiny. For instance, Andrew heard John proclaim the Messias and at once hies himself home to get Peter his brother, and together, they make their way speedily back to Christ and their destiny is attained at once. John and James came to Christ together. And when Philip saw Christ for the first time, he was not content to be selfish with his glad news either. He too went to another, and that other, Nathaniel, and announced Christ in his turn. But what a difference there is between the announcement as Andrew makes it and the way Philip speaks his glad tidings.

Andrew bursts into Peter's room and shouts his news breathlessly: "We have found the Messias." Philip, on the contrary, shows his essential character in this as in the other few incidents the Gospel records of him directly. There is nothing breathless about it; it is a matter that requires sober thought and consideration. There is no ecstasy whatever about the affair; his conviction that he has seen the Lord is a matter of evidence that satisfies his calm, dispassionate judgment. He comes to his friend Nathaniel and says quite calmly: "We have found Him of whom Moses in the law and the prophets did write, Jesus of Nazareth, the Son of Joseph." Note the details of the evidence; they show the lines of progress in the man's mind, the manner in which he was convinced that John the Baptist was no dreamy enthusiast but a trustworthy herald of the truth. Moses, in the law of the Old Testament, had spoken of a Messias to come; the prophets, during four thousand years of Jewish history, had told again and again of the circumstances and the personality of the Messias whom God had promised the fallen Adam and Eve in Eden. The Person who should come in fulfillment of those predictions must of necessity furnish His credentials; it was not a matter for enthusiastic emotion but of sober judgment. He must show that in Him and the conditions of His life were fulfilled all

the detailed prophecies of forty centuries. Philip had
evidently conned the matter very thoroughly. In his
first announcement of the Messias, he alludes to both
the Mosaic Law and the prophecies by which God
had gradually prepared His Chosen People for the acceptance of the Messias when He should make His
long-awaited appearance. Hence: "We have found
Him of whom Moses in the law and the prophets
did write, Jesus of Nazareth, the Son of Joseph." He
brings, therefore, to his friend, not only the news of
the fact, as Andrew told it to Peter; he brings the
evidence as well, detailed and carefully marshaled. He
would not only inform his friend; he would convince
as well.

The first impression of Nathaniel seems to have been
that of a good-natured, genial skeptic. He knows something of the traditions, of course; every Jew of his day
knew them well. He must have been aware that the
Messias was soon to be expected after the long wait.
He shows no manner of surprise, therefore, that Philip
should think the day has come. It is the origin of the
Messias as Philip tells it that amuses him. "Jesus of
Nazareth, Son of Joseph," Philip had said. It was to
smile, at least. Nazareth, of all places! "Can any good
come out of Nazareth?" asks Nathaniel. Then Philip
shows something of his mettle. No debating, no arguments for him. There is always the one supreme argument on which he can rely, the same one on which
Christ relied constantly, by the way, the best of all:
"Come and see." Philip had supreme confidence in the

reliability of his information. He knows that startling though it appear at first sight that anything good could possibly emanate from so notorious a place as the despicable Nazareth, still, the facts must speak for themselves and convincingly. So, "Come and see." And Nathaniel came, and saw, and was conquered for time and eternity by the personality of the Nazarene.

There came a day, some time afterward, when the crowds had followed Christ into the wastelands and were hungry. He had fed their souls on the Word of Truth; He would not do less for their bodies. Five thousand at least they were; and Christ was moved to compassion over their plight. He could not send them home unfed, for they would faint on the way, and that would have been a poor way for Him to repay their selfless devotion to Him. He turns to Philip — (one wonders just why to the sober-minded Philip) — and asks: "Whence shall we buy bread that these may eat?" Was it because Philip had established his reputation for always knowing the sober, rock-bottom facts of a case, because he was known as a practical man? Possibly. But at any rate, it is to Philip that the question was addressed. And at once comes the practical answer. "Two hundred pennyworth of bread is not sufficient for them that everyone may take a little." Note it; the amount of bread that would be required to give so great a crowd even a small lunch. Philip knew the practical facts. There was no seeming foresight of a miracle in Philip's mind. It was simply a question of something as prosaic as food supply for a crowd, and there were no commissaries at hand. The facts simply were these: It would take more than two hundred pennyworth of bread to feed them. Is it hard to imagine Christ smiling at His hardheaded Apostle? Philip had precious little imagination, it would appear, but when it was a question of practical facts, Philip knew. But there were others in the little band of Christ's friends who seem to have suspected that Christ had more in mind than a mere query about the available food supply, and the youth with his five loaves and two fishes is brought to Christ. The great miracle takes place, the thousands are fed to satiety on that ridiculously small store of food, and the world is given for all its days one of the great demonstrations that matter and space and time are subject to this Messias who has come out of the despised Nazareth.

There is another interesting light on Philip's character in the Gospel. A group of Greeks came one day to Philip — perhaps because of his own Greek name? — and asked if they might see the Master. Philip's native caution takes a hand. These are not Jews, and the Messias concerns Himself with the Chosen. What want these aliens with his great and well-loved Teacher? Still, it is not his business to reject them entirely. They knew nothing of Christ, to be sure; but who could be sure of what might not be within the plans and desires of a Teacher whose power multiplied loaves and fishes into banquets for thousands? Philip would see what could be done in the case. He goes to his friend Andrew and states the matter to him. Andrew, with characteristic decision, brings the foreigners to Christ at once. And it is easy to see in imagination the kindly eye of Christ light up as He beholds these first fruits of the Gentile harvest. They are harbingers of what is to be in days to come, when His own people will have none of Him, when they will reject their destiny despite all the centuries of prophecy, and crucify Him who came to save. It is to the Gentiles then, that He will betake Himself through His Apostles and they shall possess the kingdom of God. He said, then, in quiet joy: "The hour is come that the Son of Man should be glorified. I, if I be lifted up from the earth, will draw all things to Myself." A cryptic proclamation of Gentile vocation to God, it is true; but a proclamation none the less.

Once more Philip's name is mentioned in connection with a character-revealing incident. It is the night of the Last Supper. The traitor has been dispatched about his nefarious business; Christ is alone with His friends there. The Blessed Sacrament has been forever instituted, the First Communions have been received, one of them sacrilegiously, but the evil element had been for the time eliminated and Christ speaks lovingly and touchingly to His own. He is taking leave of them and would console them in advance and strengthen them for the ordeal that is to test their souls and try their confidence and trust in Him. He says in part: "I am the Way, and the Truth, and the Life. No man cometh to the Father but by Me. If you had known Me, you would, without doubt, have known

My Father also; and from henceforth you shall know
Him and you have seen Him." Philip is a little
puzzled, even then; all this may be clear to some of
the others, but Philip would have it further clarified;
His Master is still speaking in riddles, as far as Philip
can make out. Philip says: "Lord, show us the Father
and it is enough for us." Once again, Philip's same old
test of the truth of things; "Seeing is believing." The
answer of Christ is, as always, kindly and gentle. "Believe you not that I am in the Father and the Father
in Me; the Father who abideth in Me, He doth the
works. Believe you not that I am in the Father and the
Father in Me? Otherwise, believe for the very works'
sake. If any man love Me, he will keep My word, and
My Father will love him, and We will come to him,
and will make Our abode with him." Philip wanted to
be shown, and in good time, shown he was. He needed
time to think through the proposition, but when once
that had been done, there was no turning back. His
doubts were at an end, if doubts they deserve to be
called and not merely indications of native caution. He
believed eventually because he loved, and he loved to
the death. For like all the rest of his apostolic companions, he went forth into the highways and byways
seeking to bring in the souls of men all and sundry to
the banquet table of God's truth, and his devotion to
his mission cost him his life. But Christ came not to
destroy, but that men might have life and have it more
abundantly; Philip is conspicuously one of those who,
through their fidelity to Christ's mission, have that

life of the soul in Christ which alone can content the spirit, and have it most abundantly. Grace does not destroy native character; grace merely elevates and perfects it. Even after Pentecost, Philip became no flaming torch of heroic enthusiasm. He remained true to his innate character, a prosaic, plodding, methodical, practical man, no impetuous enthusiast, though the man's soul was aflame with personal love for Christ, but the average man instinct with a high purpose and alive with it; a noble purpose that might elevate and sublimate his character but not change it radically. It left him the sort of person he had been all his life, the average, practical man, Philip, the Prosaic.

7

MATTHEW, The Tax Collector

IT IS one of the triumphs of Christ and His religion that it so radically transforms native character. In what other religion that men have found on the earth would it be possible to find a man who wrote a whole book about events in which he played a prominent part and yet told just nothing about himself? The self-effacement of the Apostles is proverbial, certainly; not any of them surpasses Matthew in that regard, for he is one of the two Apostolic Evangelists, and yet we know almost nothing about him. His early life is largely matter for deduction from other things; his character and personality almost wholly so, and even his historical career after the Ascension is almost entirely a mystery. One thing Matthew does tell his readers of himself; it is the character of his occupation before his call to the apostolate, and he tells that, probably, just because that occupation was, in the eyes of the Jews for whom he wrote, so completely odious. Tax collectors are not, as a rule, the most popular people in any community, and Matthew was a Jewish tax collector for the Roman tyrant, and as such, specially hateful. That fact he tells; it is proof of his humility that he tells it, for the other Evangelists, in their charity to their brother-Apostle, pass over the fact in silence.

His name was Levi, his father's apparently Alpheus. He evidently lived at Capharnaum on Lake Genesareth. The town was the center of Roman government and taxation in Galilee and hence, there was stationed there a garrison with a centurion and other officers probably, as well as the civil representatives of the Roman rulers of the universe. A staff of tax gatherers there must have been, and it is probable that it was one of these subordinate positions that Levi, or Matthew, held. It is quite probable that he had heard of Christ and possibly he had even seen Him in the streets of the town, for it was Christ's own city. The fame and wonderful deeds of the "new prophet" must, therefore, have come to the ears of anybody so closely informed as the publican, Levi, was by his position compelled to be. It was part of his trade to know the state of things in the vicinity; it is hard to believe that Levi had heard nothing of Christ, though he may have dismissed the news of the Prophet as something that did not much concern him. It did concern him as a Jew, to be sure, but Levi by that time was a renegade Jew; he had to be, in order to act as a Roman tax official.

Sitting at his desk one day, however, he sees Christ approach him, and when the Lord says to him "Follow Me," there is no hesitation about it. He is at once filled with admiration for the character of Christ; possibly, Levi had seen some of the miracles of Christ in and

around Capharnaum for himself and was ardently
longing for a chance to ally himself with the Master
who had arisen in Israel. He may not have abandoned
his love for his own people, even though they hated
and scorned him as a renegade in the pay of the
Roman oppressor who made his living by oppressing
his own people in turn. At any rate, no matter what
his previous state of mind, he himself tells us that
Christ came to his side while he was sitting at the
"receipt of custom" and invited him to a rather vague
future. "Come, follow Me" he hears, and at once, leaving his position and all his earthly prospects, possibly
abandoning a very considerable fortune, certainly re-
signing a lucrative official position, he follows after the
Master, who had not whereon to lay His head. He
leaves all to follow Christ, just as readily, with the same
spontaneity of trust and confidence, as the fisherman-
Apostles of Bethsaida.

There is a significant fact about the vocation of Matthew that deserves to be noted. His call to the apostolate represents a distinct act of defiance to public
opinion on the part of Christ. Hitherto, His followers
had been chosen from the humbler walks of life. There
had been no men of wealth, no men of official position,
among those to whom that invitation to come and
follow Him had been directly spoken. Fishermen
most of them were, and such like, men of manual
labor. Christ's position was most secure as the
friend and associate of the poor among the Jews. The
time had come, it would appear, when He must point

out with public emphasis that there was no class of mankind who were to be forever excluded from His kingdom. True, He was not yet prepared to demonstrate that He had come to the Gentiles as well as to the Jews; even His Apostles were a long time in making up their minds to that. But the choice of a person so much contemned as a publican, a Roman tax collector, as one of His special friends and disciples must have come with a shock to a considerable part of the community. One wonders, incidentally, what some of the other Apostles thought of it, for they were nothing if not patriotic Jews, and it was the avowed duty and purpose of every Jew who cared for his country and its interests at all to despise and conquer the Romans and all their works and pomps whenever and wherever that might prove practicable. And here, in the public streets to make it more conspicuous, the newly announced Messias, who claimed allegiance as the King of the Jews, selects a member of the most hated class in Galilean society to act as one of His immediate company. A Roman official, to begin with, a Jewish Roman official to make matters worse, a tax collector who was regarded as battening on the misery and misfortune of others! What more despicable member of Jewish society could Christ find to call to the apostolate! That is what is implied in Matthew's humble designation of himself as a publican in the Gospel that he wrote for the Jewish converts. The other evangelists spare him that; he speaks it frankly and honestly and honorably. He must have no shade of false pretense in his glorification of his Master, who could make even the proverbial figure of Jewish contempt into a Christian Apostle and priest.

It is Matthew, too, who tells of the banquet he gave after his conversion to Christ, a banquet that Christ attended. It seems to have been a public farewell to his former friends and companions. And again the Evangelist's humility of spirit shows itself, for he states very specifically that "many publicans and sinners came and sat down with Jesus and His disciples." It is not surprising that tax-officials and sinners should be the sort of people that came to Matthew's banquet; they were the only friends Matthew had. And when the Pharisees, with their usual hypocrisy, murmured against Christ for eating with the riffraff of the town, Christ rebuked them with the consolatory words: "I came not to call the just, but sinners." That banquet marked the end of Matthew's career as a Roman official. Thereafter, he was a friend and companion of Christ in His wanderings up and down the countryside. He witnessed the mighty deeds of Christ during the rest of His public life. He saw the institution of the Blessed Eucharist and heard the divine mandate, "Do this in commemoration of Me," that made him priest along with the other Apostles. He ran away from the fracas in the Garden when Judas came, along with the others, and saw the Risen Lord after Easter as did the others. Like them, too, he carried out the preaching commission Christ had given them, and while there is no certain record that tells the time and place and manner of his death, it is traditional that he is no exception to the general rule in the ranks of the Apostles. All of them gained the martyr's palm as well as the Apostle's crown; all of them witnessed with their lives to the faith in Christ Crucified that they preached by word and example as long as either was permitted to them. That is certified to us by the ancient tradition, dating from apostolic days. The rest is silence. The little that is definitely known of him he has told us himself. His name, his occupation, his despicable friends and associates — these he records himself in his humility; the rest of his record — and it must needs, as that of an Apostle of Christ, have contained much that would have redounded to his everlasting credit among men — he conceals.

There is one salient point of his character, however, that he could not conceal in his narrative of the life of Christ, namely, his intense patriotism. His love for the Jewish people and his whole-souled devotion to their conversion from their Judaic error to Christian truth stands out in nearly every line of the Gospel that he wrote. He wrote it specifically for Jewish converts, probably before he left his own people to travel to the Gentiles who were still to be evangelized. That purpose is stamped deep on the Gospel according to St. Matthew. It was, though the original is not extant, first written in Hebrew. The genealogy, with which it opens, traces the descent of Christ through Abraham and David. The prophecies are quoted far more generously by Matthew than by any other of the Evangelists. For example, there are in Matthew's document seventy references to the Old Testament, as compared with twelve in John's. It is Matthew pre-eminently who puts the argument from the prophecies for the divinity of Christ and His mission on earth. It is Matthew who argued especially for those who had been acquainted with all those forty centuries of expectation of the Redeemer who should restore the kingdom of David and Solomon. It is he, consequently, who shows in greatest detail that the life and character and death of His Master fulfill accurately all the prophecies of the centuries concerning the Messias that God had so long ago promised.

But he is not in any sense narrow; Matthew is no bigot. He had learned the lesson of Christ's catholic mission. He closes his Gospel with the words of Christ that form the charter of the Church's universality: "Going, therefore, teach ye all nations, baptizing them in the name of the Father and of the Son and of the Holy Ghost, teaching them to observe all things whatsoever I have commanded you, and behold, I am with you all days even to the consummation of the world." Matthew had risen above the narrow interpretation of Christ's Kingdom on earth. He no longer believed, as he had once believed in good enough company, that it was the physical and political kingdom of David and Solomon that Christ had come to earth to re-establish in all its former splendor and power. He knew by that time that it was no restricted little body of men that Christ had come to save from oppression, that it was not specifically the Roman oppression He had come to overthrow, and not only the Jewish spirit He had come to liberate. He had realized thoroughly, under the tutelage of his Master, that the Kingdom of God was on the earth but not earthly, that it was the spirit of man that He had come to free through the complete truth of revealed religion, and that it was the tyranny, not of Rome, but of Satan and hell that He had come to break. Hence, the apostolic career that had begun in nationalistic narrowness of outlook closed on the universal note. The man who had begun as a collector of Roman taxes in Galilee ended as a preacher of the universal kingdom of Christ among men, teaching them to observe all things that his Master had taught him.

8

NATHANIEL, The Guileless

THERE is more than one of the Twelve Apostles of whom little is known for certain. There is scarcely one, however, of whom there is so very little known as Nathaniel. Even his name, and, of course, consequently, his antecedents and his personal character, are matters of debate. There is in his case even an apparent disagreement between the Gospel according to St. John, on the one hand, and the three Synoptic Gospels, on the other. The latter call him Bartholomew; John, when he mentions this Apostle at all, calls him Nathaniel. They were not two different people, however. Bartholomew means Son of Tolmai, and the Apostle is so called to point out his Hebraic origin at least. That much we may safely deduce from the surname, that he was a Jew. He appears to have resided in or near Bethsaida, like so many others of the Apostolic College. What his occupation may have been is a mystery; the Gospel tells nothing of that. That he was a man of considerable culture and education seems a logical deduction from his action and his mode of speech, though that is slender basis for argument when

quoting from documents that so honestly bear the
mark of the human writer upon them. The outstanding fact about him before his call to the apostolate is
the friendship that bound him to Philip, the sober,
matter-of-fact Apostle. As Philip's friend, Nathaniel
had, of course, heard considerable of John the Baptist.
He knew that Philip was attracted to the Baptist's
preaching on the Jordan, knew the essential of the
preacher's message; namely, that the time of the
Messias was at hand and that the Chosen People must
prepare for His advent by fasting and penance.
Whether he was himself very much impressed with
the Baptist, whether he was even curious enough to go
out from the town to the riverside where John did
most of his preaching to see for himself what sort of
preacher this was that was causing so great a sensation
and arousing even his friend Philip from some of his
cautious reserve, does not appear in the Gospel record
of him. It is no great stretch of historical imagination,
however, to see Nathaniel in the crowd that John addressed so vehemently; it is not absurd to suppose that
his upright and honest soul was stirred, to some degree
at least, by the strenuous message of this preacher of
penance. At any rate, he does not seem to have been at
all surprised when Philip came to him one evening
and told him quite calmly and soberly as was his wont,
that the great event of the Messias's coming had taken
place and that the Baptist had that day pointed out the
Redeemer to those about him, proclaiming Him the
Lamb of God.

It was a sober enough announcement for Philip to make of that wonderful event. Four thousand years, at least, the tradition had been kept alive; for forty centuries men had yearned and longed for that day; prophets all that length of time had seen the Person of the Messias in vision and related striking details of His personality, His life, His descent, His mode of death. It was the one great event on which the mind of the religious Jew of that day was centered; it could never have been long from the consciousness of any Jew that knew the traditions, for the signs all pointed to the fulfillment of the prophecies some years before, and it was no new idea to present itself, that somewhere the Messias should by that day already be upon the earth. And yet, when Philip had seen the Redeemer and satisfied his careful, inquiring, sober judgment that there was no mistake about it, what a phlegmatic announcement he makes of it to his friend Bartholomew! Andrew, under similar conditions, breaks out into a shout to tell his brother Peter; Philip's announcement of the glad tidings for which all had waited so long is almost a theological argument! "We have found Him of whom Moses in the law, and the prophets did write, Jesus of Nazareth, the Son of Joseph." There is no enthusiasm evident there; it is not the speech of a fanatic of any sort. Philip quotes Moses in the Law, alludes to the Prophets, names the Messias, tells His Father's name, and even His place of residence! All that in one sentence, and the first sentence in which he tells his closest friend the greatest news that earth had known. But he seems to have known his friend thoroughly.

Nathaniel was no wild-eyed enthusiast, either; he is just as dispassionate, just as judicial in his attitude of mind when confronted with the great news as is Philip who heralds it to him. He speaks that sentence that contains a wealth of meaning, a sentence that sounds uncomfortably like a sneer. "Can anything good come out of Nazareth?" He is dubious, apparently, about the reality of the asserted Messias. He has probably read the records of his own people and the doings of alleged prophets till he is forcedly cautious about accepting a new prophet. There had been false Messiases, more than one, and it is not to be wondered at that Nathaniel should be cautious. He does not at once deny that Christ is the Promised of God; he is too just-minded for that. After all, it is too important a matter to be dogmatic in rejection of it. He smilingly replies to his convinced friend, casting as it were a dash of cold water on the conviction of Philip. Nazareth was a notorious place, despised among the towns of Galilee. And now he, Nathaniel, is asked to believe that from that very town the great Redeemer of the Chosen People has sprung! It was like expecting great culture and refinement from Main Street; only worse! "Can anything good come out of Nazareth?" asks Nathaniel, and Philip argues about it not at all. He takes the only possible course with people like Nathaniel who want to be shown before they believe; he uses a most convincing argument. He says simply and quietly; "Come and see." And Nathaniel went, and saw, and believed.

When the Saviour saw the two friends coming, He seems to have said not one word to the faithful Philip, but He did say to those about Him of Nathaniel, "Behold an Israelite indeed in whom there is no guile." Nathaniel seems to have heard the speech of Christ and knew from it that he was known to Christ. He wants to know how that has come about, and Christ favors him with an explanation. "Before that Philip called thee, when thou wast under the fig tree, I saw thee." There is a mystery here. The Evangelist, St. John, who reports this beautiful scene between Christ and the two Apostles, says nothing whatever of any fig tree. Christ seems to allude here to some incident that Nathaniel would certainly remember and recognize but which no one else in the company knew. For at once, Nathaniel makes his remarkable profession of faith. "Rabbi, Thou art the Son of God, Thou art the King of Israel." He had been a skeptic, it is true; he had questioned, apparently condescendingly at least, the possibility of anything worth talking about coming out of despicable Nazareth; he had been prevailed upon by the conviction of his friend to come to see for himself. And at once, at the very first contact with Christ, the Saviour privileges him with a very special demonstration of superhuman powers by reminding him of some incident that took place under a fig tree when no human eye had seen him.

It is a privilege accorded none of the others so soon in their relationship with Christ. None of the others speaks so definitely and decisively his faith in the divinity of Christ. To the others, Christ is their Friend and Master, the Promised of God, and no more, apparently, for a long time. To Nathaniel it is given to reach the heights of faith at one bound and to proclaim his faith immediately. He is forced to realize that a Man who could tell him of the fig-tree episode was endowed with more than human powers. He breaks forth then in his beautiful and confident avowal: "Thou art the Son of God, Thou art the King of Israel." It took considerable time and experience with the wonders Christ wrought to bring the others to that stage of trusting faith. The new convert speaks his faith in Christ's divinity at the first meeting. Why the difference? Whence this sublime attainment of faith at one bound? The others reached that faith through love and knowledge; Nathaniel seems to have been overwhelmed with it in a moment of supernatural enlightenment through the glimpse permitted him of Christ's divine nature. The praise of Christ suggests a possible reason.

Before even Philip had presented his friend to the Messias whom he had found, Christ set the stamp of infallible approval on the character of the neophyte. Seeing Nathaniel approaching under the guidance of Philip, our Lord speaks those words that reveal so much of the beautiful spirit and character of Nathaniel. "Behold an Israelite indeed in whom there is no guile." What a noble soul those words require to justify them! They were spoken, so far as revelation has been

vouchsafed us, of no other human being. The angel of
God salutes Mary as full of grace, it is true. Christ
Himself says of the Baptist that greater man was never
born of woman. The Holy Ghost expresses much of
the greatness of St. Joseph when he is called, in noble
simplicity, a just man. But of no other of the Apostles
do we have any such encomium of Christ's. Peter He
made His representative on earth and the head of the
Apostles. John was His beloved disciple whom He
favored with the custody of His Mother. James the
Greater was privileged to see both Tabor and Gethsemani. But not even these receive any such specific
verbal praise as the obscure and lowly Nathaniel; he is
the Israelite without guile. That designation remains
the greatest badge of his earthly distinction. To be so
pure, so honest, so noble and upright that even Christ
Himself is constrained to proclaim him guileless is the
great distinction of Nathaniel. And it speaks volumes
for his character. There can have been nothing whatever in the man suggestive of craft or conceit; a lie for
him was just impossible. He was honest to the core,
with that intellectual honesty that is most rare. He
was a simple soul and strong. No crannies or shadowy
corners wherein guilty secrets might lurk, no decep-
tions of self or others, no shade of the dishonorable
could there be in such a soul that dared to bring itself
face to face with the All-seeing. The soul of the man
must have been pure white light, glowing and lumi-
nous with all the virtues; he was the one Israelite without guile.

His future history in the seminary of Christ is a matter of a line or two. After the Resurrection, Christ showed Himself to several of His followers on the lakeshore. There were present on that occasion Simon Peter, and Thomas who is called Didymus, and Nathaniel, the sons of Zebedee, and two others of the disciples. They fished all night but in vain; they caught nothing, the Sacred Writer tells us. In the morning, Jesus stood on the shore but they knew Him not. He told them to cast the net once more, this time from the right side of the ship, with wonderful results in a draught of fishes that they could scarcely manage. In their success, Peter read the answer to the riddle. "It is the Lord," he cried, and wrapping himself hastily in his cloak, he cast himself into the waters to be sooner with his Master. Jesus ate with them then, there on the shore of the lake, and after the meal, gave Peter in the presence of others his great commission to feed the lambs and the sheep of the Christian flock. In that momentous scene, Nathaniel is silent. His part then as always was to listen and to love.

But after Pentecost had driven fear of the Jews from the hearts of the Apostles and their missionary work was so nobly begun, Nathaniel bore his part of his labors of the day and the heats with the others. The scene of his labors in the cause of Christ Crucified is unknown, though traditions of more or less weight see him preaching and praying and laboring in nearly every section of Asia. The mode of his death is no better known, though traditional Christian art represents him as having been flayed alive somewhere in Armenia. These things, with plenty of others that we should be interested in knowing, are reserved for revelation on the Great Day of Reckoning when the Sign of the Son of Man shall appear in the heavens and the triumphant Christ shall appear with great power and majesty. But there is one verdict of His, then, that can be confidently foreseen now. He will find no other thing to say of Nathaniel than the beautiful thing He said in Galilee: "Behold an Israelite indeed in whom there is no guile."

9

THOMAS, The Skeptic

IT IS not only a man's virtues that give us an insight into his inmost character; his vices sometimes produce the same enlightening effect. The Apostle Thomas is a case in point, for he is known more fully and profoundly through what we know of his faults than through his unquestionable virtues. It is a strange thing that the good things to be said of Thomas must be so largely deduced from the fact that he was chosen by Christ as an Apostle at all, while the faults of the man are told rather explicitly. From the viewpoint of historical certainty, there is very little known of Thomas's early life. The Synoptic Gospels merely mention him among the Twelve; it is in the Gospel according to St. John that we get a glimpse into his soul and character. He would appear to be a Galilean, like most of the Apostles, but what his origin and antecedents may have been is a matter of conjecture. Whether he was one of those of whom tradition says that they could neither read nor write, or whether he had acquired something of culture and education through contact with the Greek and Roman civilization that was spread along the shores of Lake Genesa-reth, is again a mystery. He is called Didymus in the Gospels, meaning "twin." The name Thomas in Syriac means "twin." His parentage is unknown, and the name of his twin is likewise lost in the mists of anti-quity. We simply do not know, and the Holy Spirit, in His inspiration of the Gospel narratives, has seen fit to preserve that mystery. There are but three instances recorded in the Inspired Writings of Thomas's acts and speech, but they are all three of them highly signifi-cant. All of them occur in the Gospel according to St. John, and each of them may serve us as little bones serve the scientist in his reconstruction of the whole skeleton of a long-forgotten beast. These three little bits of information that we have of Thomas through the Gospel are enough to show us something of the heart and spirit of the man; his character speaks through them most eloquently and revealingly.

The first of them shows Thomas a man of supreme courage and self-sacrifice. It is the occasion when Christ announced to His disciples that He would return to Judea to visit His friend Lazarus. The Apostles little needed to be told what risk that involved. From every human standpoint, it was most highly imprudent. The risk was enormous. The populace had just very re-cently risen against Christ in one of those periodic outbursts of mob-spirit like that which was destined to compass His death. They tried to stone Christ, and it was only because His hour had not yet come that He employed His divine power to escape their ire. It had

all happened just a little while before. And now the
Apostles hear their beloved Master calmly announce
His intention of going straight back to the danger
from which He had so lately escaped. The risk was
great, and the Apostles knew it was great. It was a risk
that Christ's friends and companions must needs share,
for it was enough to arouse the angry passion of that
mob against any man to be recognized as a friend of
Christ's. The project, humanly speaking, looked downright mad. It was as much as a man's life was worth
to go back just then. And yet, back Christ would go.
To be sure, the faith and confidence of the Apostles in
Christ and His power to protect Himself and them
should have stood more testing than that; they were
not yet the miracles of grace and superhuman heroism
they later became. They thought more of the danger
than of the Protector they should have. It was death
they faced, and they were no heroes. But on that occasion, Thomas rose to his opportunity. He spoke,
shortly, concisely, to the point unquestionably. Christ,
as it were, closed the debate, saying: "Let us go to him
[Lazarus]." Thomas then said to his companions in
the apostolate: "Let us also go, that we may die with
Him." There spoke supreme courage and devotion.
With Thomas it is no longer a question of avoiding
death or worse, no question now of protection, human
or divine. There is just one thing to be done, as he sees
it, one demand of friendship and apostleship; if Christ
is to go to His death, the Apostles, plainly and simply,
must die with Him.

And so they went off, the devoted little company, along with their great Friend and Master, thinking of nothing else but the death they were to meet in His company. But that, in the designs of Christ, was to be not yet. He went and raised Lazarus in the conditions known so well. And there can be little of doubt about the purpose Christ had in view in that remarkable miracle. Aside even from the unmistakable announcement He made at the graveside of His intentions, even before the journey to Bethany was started, Christ had said to His Apostles when He told them that Lazarus was dead: "Lazarus our friend sleepeth, but I go that I may awake him out of sleep." The Apostles, with their usual shortsightedness at that period of their training in Christ's college of souls, thought He meant a natural sleep, and said so, arguing from the fact that there was no need to face the dangers of the journey. Christ then assured them that Lazarus is dead, and goes on to say: "And I am glad for your sakes that I was not there, that you may believe; but let us go to him." He went, and the Apostles bravely and nobly went with Him, and the world and they were given that stupendous miracle that should have convinced all mankind that the Person whose command death itself obeys must needs be Lord and God. And to that effect, the noble courage of Thomas contributed materially, for it cannot have failed to strengthen the courage of his companions. It is so simple and so lofty: "Let us also go that we may die with Him." True, when the test of dying with Him did arise, Thomas, like the rest, failed Him. But it was a failure to be expiated later in a martyr's heroism.

The next time Thomas appears by name in the pageant of the Gospel he acts in keeping with the traditional character he has assumed through the centuries of Christian history. It is on the occasion of the Last Supper, during Christ's last touching address to His friends. He is taking His leave of those whom He has associated with Himself during three years of significant friendship. "I go to prepare a place for you," He says, "and whither I go you know, and the way you know." Should it still have been so mysterious to them what He meant? He had told them time and again that His hour was at hand, that it was incumbent on Him to return to the Father who sent Him. But their education was still incomplete; the Paraclete had not yet been sent. It is dark and mysterious to them still, and Thomas speaks his mind once more. No questioning now of the others, no comparing opinions. He hears his Lord tell of leaving them to go by a way that He says they know; Thomas is not aware of knowing it, and he would have no misunderstandings. He says so. "Lord, we know not whither Thou goest, and how can we know the way?" It is a pathetic speech, thrilling with devotion and love of the man who saw his great Friend and Master going from him into the unknown, whither he was expected sometime to follow. The way was dark, and Thomas far from home. He would have Christ lead on, and more explicitly. His question elicited this great answer: "I am the Way and the Truth and the Life; no man cometh to the Father but by Me." Thomas can hardly have grasped the full significance of the answer. Philip, the Prosaic, certainly did not, and Christ goes on in greater detail and explicitness to reassure the hearts fainting at the prospect of separation from Him: "I will not leave you orphans, I will come to you; peace I leave with you, My peace I give unto you; let not your heart be troubled nor let it be afraid."

One other incident in Thomas's life, and only one other, is recorded in the Gospel, the incident that has fastened to the Apostle's name the epithet by which he is most generally known. "Doubting Thomas" has become a proverbial phrase in more than one language to this day. It is taken as an expression of reproach, and yet it is not so entirely sure as that would seem to imply, that the skepticism, the doubting disposition of Thomas's mind, is entirely blameworthy. True, it elicited a mild rebuke from Christ, but a loving one none the less. The Apostles were locked in the Upper Chamber of the Last Supper, after Christ's death, for fear of the Jews, and plenty of reason they had to be afraid, to be sure. The spirit of mob violence was still ripe in the town, filled to bursting as it was with visitors who had little to do all day or night but stand around public squares and street corners looking for excitement or pastime. That mob had murdered Christ just a little while before; anyone recognized as a disciple and follower of His would certainly not be long in treading the same road to his own Calvary.

To that little company, gathered there in seclusion and in terror, appears Christ, gloriously risen and resplendent. We are specifically told that Thomas was not with the rest. Why not? What business could have torn him from the others? Where was he? Out in the city somewhere on business of some sort? Out to look over the situation in the city to learn if it is yet safe for the Apostles and Mary to venture out? Who knows? Who will ever know? At any rate, he was missing, apparently the only one of the remaining eleven that was missing on that great day. He returned soon after and was told of the great event, Christ's resurrection and His appearance there in their midst. He is the skeptic still. Why should he not have believed? What right had he, of all people, to reject the unanimous testimony of the others? They joyously announced that they had had the best of the tests; they had seen, and proverbially, "seeing is believing." Not enough for Thomas. "Except I shall see in His hands the print of the nails and put my finger into the place of the nails, and put my hand into His side, I will not believe." It is the height of audacity, of course. The rest of them had demanded no such proof; they saw and believed. Even seeing was not enough for Thomas; he must touch and feel as well. Why should he have been so hard to convince? It could not have been because it was an unexpected development; Christ had told them repeatedly that He would rise from the dead and carry out the rest of His earthly mission. It should have been easy for Thomas to believe, since it was precisely what he had been taught to expect. But he is one big doubt; he will not believe unless the Person he has come to believe is God Himself, submits to little tests of his own devising. It is the one great instance in apostolic history of the scientific spirit; Thomas at least must be shown, and God Himself submit His risen body to scientific demonstrations before this one of the Twelve is convinced. He has his way of it, remarkably enough. Christ very obligingly submits to his requirements, appears again in their midst when Thomas is with the rest, and calls the skeptic to His side to apply the test. "He saith to Thomas: put in thy finger hither and see My hands, and bring hither thy hand and put it into My side, and be not faithless but believing."

That speech of Christ's should have been enough in itself to convince even a thorough skeptic like Thomas, and it would seem at least possible that it did just that. There is nothing in the sacred text to indicate that Thomas did actually apply his tests when the chance was offered him. The mere fact that Christ should have known of the test Thomas required should have been sufficient to demonstrate supernatural powers of knowledge on our Lord's part, if nothing more. The Evangelist says nothing of that; he does not in any sense indicate that Thomas used his fingers as he was bidden. The response of the Apostle's noble soul is immediate, it would appear, without further demonstration: "My Lord and my God." It is a noble and significant profession of faith from the faithless. Thomas exclaims "my Lord," indicating that he is entirely con-

vinced that it is really the Lord he had known before
Calvary that he sees before him in that Upper Chamber. But he does not stop there; he has gone far past
the scientific stage now: "My Lord and my God" he
exclaims, proclaiming to all the world for all time to
come that he, Thomas, the Skeptic, is entirely convinced that the Christ who had been murdered on
Friday had risen on Sunday superior to the grave and
that that fact proves Him God. With a gentle forgiving
smile, surely, Christ said to him: "Because thou hast
seen, Thomas, thou hast believed; blessed are they who
have not seen and have believed."

And there, probably, the significance of Thomas's
doubting mind and the demonstration of Christ's divinity that it achieved, is indicated. It was not only to
convince Thomas who was thus allowed to see for
himself that Christ so appeared; it was to convince
millions in afterdays who would not see and yet were
expected to believe. It would seem that our Lord de-
liberately anticipated some of the objections other
doubting Thomases would make in later centuries. The
scientific spirit, so called, would have to be shown; it
would refuse to believe unless Christ would submit
Himself to scientific tests of its own invention. Miracles, and prophecies, and preaching the Gospel to the
poor would mean nothing to a certain class of mind
in years to come; those minds would see and feel and
weigh and test scientifically. It was not to be given
them personally so to test the Risen Christ; Thomas
was their representative. He inspects the body of Christ,

he is permitted to feel and touch and handle it, if he sees fit so to do. There can be no further question about the reality of that body that so submitted itself to scientific test; it was a genuine body, not a specter, that Thomas saw before him, of a certainty. It was the same body that had been crucified. There can, therefore, for all the ages of time, be no further questioning about that fact. Christ did rise from the dead, and therefore, the cornerstone of the whole edifice of things Christian, the divinity of Christ, stands impregnable to all the winds that blow. Men may doubt and men may deny Christ, as men have always doubted and denied. The fact remains that Thomas saw and perhaps felt the risen body of the Crucified Christ and Thomas made his act of faith on the spot. Thomas saw and believed, and all the Thomases ever since can do no more in reason than win for themselves Christ's encomium: "Blessed are they who have not seen and have believed."

10

BRETHREN OF THE LORD

THE persistence of the physical blood relationship of brotherhood among the Twelve is remarkable. There were no fewer than seven of the Twelve Apostles who could claim another of the company as bloodbrother: Peter and Andrew, James and John, and at the other end of the list, three brothers; namely, James the Less, Jude, and Simon the Zealot. It is of these men that the Gospel speaks in the expression that styles them "the brethren of the Lord." It is a mode of expression that has given rise to plenty of misunderstanding and not a little false accusation of one sort and another. The virginity of the Blessed Virgin has been attacked again and again because of that expression, but quite mistakenly. It is not to be taken in the strict sense of the English word "brother" when these three men, and their other brother Joseph, who was not favored with membership among the Twelve, are called the brethren of the Redeemer, for Christ's brothers, in the sense of having the same parents, they unquestionably were not. There is a tradition, but not a reliable one, that they were children of St. Joseph by a former marriage, but that does not square with the universal tradition from most ancient times that Joseph, like the other members of the Holy Family, was a virgin. The four brothers in question were cousins of Christ's, and not directly first cousins either. They were sons of Cleophas, who was a brother of St. Joseph, and of Mary, a cousin of the Blessed Virgin. These two worthy people, Cleophas and Mary, had two daughters as well, Mary and Salome, and the latter of these is usually taken to be the wife of Zebedee, and the mother of the Sons of Thunder, James and John. It is of these two women, Mary and Salome, that the Jews spoke when they asked: "Are not also His sisters here with us?" So that at least five of the Twelve Apostles were related in various degrees of kindred with their Master, and these three obscure men, James the Less, and Jude Thaddeus, and Simon Zealotes are brothers, one of another, and cousins of Christ.

Before their call to the dignity of the apostolate, these relatives of our Lord's evinced nothing like enthusiasm for Him or His mission. They seem rather to have been hostile to Him. And even after they became Apostles, they were long in arousing anything like ardent or enthusiastic support of Christ in their souls. For example, just seven months before the Crucifixion they reproached Christ for not manifesting Himself to the world. St. John says: "They did not believe in Him," and while it would not be accurate to suppose they had no faith at all in Christ — they must have had or they would not have remained with Him — still, it is pain-

fully true that they had nothing of the flaming enthusiasm in His regard that some of the others had.
They were still, even at that late day — and after it —
looking for the sensational establishment of Christ's
earthly kingdom. They still hoped and expected that
He would somehow drive the hated Romans from
Judea and Galilee and establish once more the splendor
and greatness of the pristine Jewish kingdom of David
and Solomon. Even at the Last Supper that hope had
not entirely been transformed into something greater
and finer because more spiritual. Even then, Jude asks
the Saviour: "Lord, how is it that Thou wilt manifest
Thyself to us and not to the world?" Shortsighted
Apostle! He was querulous about his greatest honor
and privilege, and complained because the world did
not share it with him! He still longed somewhat for
the fleshpots that he saw passing from him and his
company if Christ held to the plan He seemed to be
announcing to them there on that solemn occasion.
Jude, along with the others, was to change his mind
finally, but it took a long time to do it, took as well the
great events of the Passion and Calvary and Easter
morning to effect the change in his outlook on his own
future and on Christ's. In due time, after the descent
of the Paraclete, Jude and his brothers in the apostolate
did finally realize the significance of that warning of
Christ's that His Kingdom was to be in this world but
not of the world. And once confirmed in grace, of
course, there was no faltering in Jude or in any of the
rest of the Apostles. Jude Thaddeus was a man of quick

intelligence and generous spirit when once fully convinced, but it seems to have required Pentecost to seal his soul to the spiritual kingdom that Christ came to found on earth. Jude persisted a long time in an illusion, but that derogates nothing from his fidelity and devotion to Christ, his Friend and Lord. And there was something both of intimate fraternal love and of chivalrous devotion in Jude's adherence to our Saviour.

It is traditional that after Pentecost, Simon the Zealot and Jude preached the Gospel in Arabia. Brothers in everything else, they were associated in their apostolic work and they were not separated even in death. For together they attracted first the admiration and awe, and then the hatred, of the enemies of the Gospel in Arabia, and on the same day, they paid the penalty of their devotion to their Lord when they refused to renounce Christ and offer incense to the pagan godlings. Simon, tradition will have it, was sawed in halves and Jude beheaded.

Of the personal character of Simon, the Gospel speaks almost nothing. There is little that he did or said that has been preserved in the inspired writings of the New Testament. But the Gospel does call him the Zealot, and that appelation may stand for his political affiliations as well as for a sign of his personal characteristics. He represents, as it were, in the Apostolic College, the militant patriot. He had been a member of the sect known as the Zealots whose ambition and purpose it was to keep aflame the patriotic spirit of the Jews. He was a fiery patriot and had apparently fought against the Roman invader in more ways than one. Whether his brothers were also members of the same sect is unknown; perhaps they were. Simon is specifically designated as the Zealot, and surely it is no mistake to see more than a chance sect name in the designation. His fiery zeal was not entirely for the Jewish kingdom; it was transferred to the person of Christ. One indication of it is in the narrative concerning the Last Supper. When Christ says, sadly: "Let us go hence to meet the traitor," Simon bursts out with the observation: "Lord, here are two swords." The Jewish patriot spoke there, but with what a difference! Probably he had not as yet entirely overcome his longing desire for the terrestrial kingdom of Christ, but at all events, his fighting spirit was aroused by the thought of the danger impending over the head of his devoted Lord through the treason of Judas, and he would resist. "Lord, here are two swords," he says, but it remained for not him but a namesake to make use of one of them in physical defense of Christ that Christ did not at all desire. The spirit was there, at any rate, and if it was wrongly directed, the fault was not of the heart but the head. He was a man of warmhearted devotion to his great Friend, and while he was no hero till after Pentecost, still, the spiritual temperature of the Apostolic Body must have been raised materially by his accession.

Jude and Simon Zelotes do not seem to have been objects of any special affection or preference on our Lord's part either before or after the Resurrection. It

was otherwise with their brother, James. St. Paul is at
some pains to point out the superior position of James
the Little. He was given one of the first visions of the
Risen Saviour. Tradition has it that he was appointed
bishop of Jerusalem by our Lord Himself. Whether
that be true or not matters little; what is beyond disputing is his special position, and it is a position of
special authority in Jerusalem. A difference of opinion
arose among the Apostles and the other Christians soon
after the work of preaching the Gospel had gathered
something like a crowd of converts. They were all Jews
formerly, but now some Gentiles had seen the light of
faith and were followers of Christ. The question arose
as to whether they had first to fulfill the requirements
of the Jewish Law. The Apostles and other ancients
assembled to discuss the matter. Peter and Paul gave
their opinions; the next was James's. He was held in
special esteem by all the Christians, Jews and Gentiles
alike. The Jews regarded him highly as a strict follower of the ancient tradition, not any longer now as
necessary, but as a matter of traditional practice on the
Apostle's part. His austerity, his wisdom, his meekness,
his mildness of treatment of other people while most
austere with himself, all made him an object of special
affection on the part of the Christians of the Holy City.
His name became a badge of special distinction to
those associated with him. It is interesting to note it in
the Sacred Writings. For example, in Luke, Jude is
simply the brother of James; in Matthew and Mark,
the wife of Cleophas is called Mary, mother of James

the Less; in St. Paul, he is, by pre-eminence, the brother of the Lord; Jude himself, in his Epistle, immediately after proclaiming his title of "servant of Jesus Christ," calls himself "brother of James."

The persecution in the year 42 drove the rest of the Apostles abroad over the earth; James remained behind as the Bishop of Jerusalem. Herod Agrippa, the petty little princeling who held his shadowy authority in the kingdom of the Jews through the support of Caligula and Claudius as long as he would do what he was told, murdered James the Greater. Like the sycophant he was, he was anxious to further his claims on the Jews whom he had pleased with that murder by slaughtering his namesake, James the Little, as well. But Providence watched over the Bishop of Jerusalem and postponed his martyr's dignity for twenty years. The crown was accorded him then, at the age of eighty-six, when he was flung from the top of a tower for proclaiming the divinity of Christ. He struggled to rise to his knees to pray, like Stephen, for his murderers, when a blow on the head sent his great soul to God.

Ancient tradition relates one little fact of James that floods his character with light. His Epistle reveals him as a man of calm mind, trust in Christ, a man of prayer and devotion to the poor. Tradition says of him that he had prayed so much and so long that his knees were calloused like a camel's. He was not surnamed "The Just" for nothing. His austerity was remarkable, even in that age of heroic austerity. It is said of him that he drank no wine, ate no animal food, used no razor, did not anoint himself with fragrant oils as was and is the custom of the Orient, and that he spent days and nights on his knees in prayer for the needs of his people and the conversion of the world to the Christ who had won his own allegiance so entirely. The little scraps of information we have of his character are distressingly meager, but they are enough to paint an unmistakable picture of the man as the true follower of Christ and the genuine apostolic bishop.

11

JUDAS, The Man of Lost Opportunity

THE name Judas was a common name among the Jews, so common, in fact, that there were two of the Twelve who bore it: Jude who is surnamed Thaddeus, and Judas, the Traitor, of Keriot. It is to distinguish the traitor from the faithful Apostle that the Scripture invariably mentions the sinister Judas with the addition either of some reference to the treason that perpetuates his name to all time in execration, or else to his birthplace, Keriot. There is a possible significance in that birthplace, incidentally, for it marks out Judas as the only one of the original Twelve who was not a Galilean. Keriot was a town in Judea, and Judas Iscariot, consequently, the only Judean in the apostolic company of Christ's friends. Of his antecedents, his personal characteristics in early life, his training, his parentage, his friends, his occupation, his likes and dislikes, his instinctive mental and spiritual reactions — of all these we know just nothing. The Scriptures tell nothing of it all. The Evangelists are entirely silent about the circumstances of his call to the apostolate; we find him enumerated among the twelve, always at the foot of the list; that, and no more. His elevation to the apostolic dignity, his treachery after a few incidents that throw floods of light into the dark places of that sinister soul, and the mode of his death — that sums up the Bible history of Judas, who has made his name a symbol of everything despicable. There is in any language of modern times no more hated insult than that implied in the attribution of his name. It was not always thus with the name of Judas. It was once a heroic name; it stood in Jewish history for one of the finest and noblest of manly characters, one of the nation's great, God-raised heroes. For all time, however, since the treason of the Apostle, the name is in execration.

It is not easy for a modern who has been educated and trained in the Christian tradition to do justice to the early character of Judas, the Traitor. We are inclined to allow the later history of the man to color our appreciation of his character before his elevation to apostolic dignity. That may be quite accurate, as a matter of fact, but it is scarcely provable that he was always despicable. True, the Sacred Writer somewhere says he was a liar from the beginning; it may have been from the beginning of his career as an Apostle. At any rate, if he were always all-wicked, it would be difficult to explain his choice by the all-seeing Christ as one of His special friends. It seems more reasonable to suppose that he had his good qualities, just as the others had their weaknesses. There is nothing to be gained from any viewpoint in exaggerating either the moral exaltation of the saints or yet the degradation of a Judas. It still remains true that no human being is or ever was entirely bad; such a man never lived, and Judas was essentially a human being. Wicked, it is true, despicable beyond the imagination of ordinary men and women, a liar and thief and hypocrite as well as a traitor — these things he was at the close of his life. Who shall lift for us the veil in which his youth and early manhood are concealed and show us what manner of man he was when he left his father's house to make his career in the world? Who shall tell what sort of man he was when Christ, for inscrutable reasons of His own, chose him from among thousands of better men for the honor and privilege of His special company? Mystery these things are and mysterious they must remain, barring special revelation, till the Day of Doom, when he, with the rest of mankind, will appear before the Judgment Seat of the Redeemer in the eye of the world.

It has been suggested that the fact that Judas was an alien among the Twelve had something to do with his subsequent career, because it produced a lack of sympathy between himself and the rest of the Apostles. That can scarcely be true, for we are specifically told by St. John that Judas carried the common purse, and surely men, even apostolic men, do not trust their closest approach to earthly wealth to men of whom they are in any way suspicious. He was the treasurer of the company, administering what scanty funds they had or acquired in their wanderings about the country-

side in the company of Christ. It would seem to have
been Judas's duty to transact the business of the apostolic body and pay the expenses they incurred in their
travels. It would have been thoroughly easy, therefore,
for Judas to have made himself an embezzler, as we
should call him today, by appropriating to himself
some of the common funds. It would seem that is the
sense of the Evangelist's assertion that Judas was a
thief. It would have been all the more easy, since the
rest of the Apostles, having to a greater or less degree
abandoned earthly pursuits and interests, must have
been even less inclined to suspicion of one of their own
number than ordinary men would have been. Why
should they have mistrusted Judas? Had not Christ
chosen him just as He had chosen the rest of the
twelve? That would certainly be passport enough with
the Apostles. Judas was trusted. Judas was recreant to
that trust, and the man who would defraud his own
brethren and friends, banded together in an enterprise
that more than once must have looked like a forlorn
hope, is despicable indeed. We have the best of author-
ities for believing Judas was of that caliber. It would
seem that there is even worse to be said in this item of
the indictment against Judas's moral character. One of
the sins crying to heaven for vengeance is defrauding
the poor. Judas is guilty. Guilty, not only because
Christ and the Apostles were the poorest of the poor
— for did not Christ Himself say He had not whereon
to lay His head? — but guilty, likewise, because
through his peculations the alms for the poor of the

land were necessarily stinted. A man must be low indeed to steal from beggars and widows and orphans, from the destitute and helpless generally. Judas did it, and systematically.

Along with that dishonesty, there was another and a worse variety of dishonesty, the intellectual sort; for Judas was hypocrite as well as liar and thief. We read of him protesting against expenditure, and attributing his opposition to miserably lying motives. On the great occasion when Mary Magdalene signified her repentance for her misdeeds by pouring over the Sacred Person of Christ the contents of a costly ampulla of fragrant oil, it is Judas who murmurs against the "waste." St. John tells it thus: "Then one of His disciples, Judas Iscariot, he that was about to betray Him, said: Why was not this ointment sold for three hundred pence and given to the poor? Now he said this, not because he cared for the poor; but because he was a thief, and having the purse, carried the things that were put therein." Significant narration, in terse words! Note the connection apparent in the Evangelist's mind between Judas's miserliness and hypocrisy, and his treason to Christ. He protested, St. John says tersely and baldly enough, not because he cared for the poor, they were the least of his concern, but because he was a thief. He saw three hundred pence expended in ointment instead of put into his purse; his miserly soul lusted for those pence, and he betrayed himself in speech that reveals his inmost character in all its hideous littleness. On that occasion, Christ must have spoken to the hypocritical Apostle as well as to the scribes and Pharisees to whom He addressed His stinging rebuke: "The poor you have always with you, Me you have not always." Was there not there a silent invitation to the brooding, money-bound soul of Judas to rise from his degradation as Mary had risen from hers? "Me you have not always" may well have meant in Christ's mind far more than a reminder of His impending death. To Judas, however, it meant nothing, or less than nothing. It was one of the great opportunities for better and nobler things that Judas was constantly missing.

His hypocrisy went on apace, however, as he fell from one depth of degradation to another. It would not be difficult to see significance in the close connection in the Gospels between the murmuring of Judas at the feast in Bethania and the treason. In Matthew and Mark, the narrative goes immediately from one to the other, from the scene when Judas missed his chance to rise out of his fallen self, to that other scene that marks the climax of even Judas's transgressions. He went to the high priests, he, of the Chosen Twelve, to see how good a bargain he could make for the betrayal that his fiendish soul had concocted. He, not the priests, took the initiative in the hideous business; it is the Apostle, not the Jewish priests and their hangers-on, that is primarily blamable in the horrible transaction. To them it was a mere matter of business, dirty business to be sure, but why should they be particularly squeamish about the methods they used to attain their end if one of Christ's own selected friends was not above such bargaining? The bartering goes on and finally Judas consents to sell the person of his Lord and Benefactor for thirty pieces of silver, about twelve dollars and a half, according to one calculation.

Opportunity to consummate the treachery is not long coming. Christ gathers His friends about Him for the final feast, a love-feast if ever there was one, and Judas invited like the rest, pollutes the spiritual atmosphere with the presence of his guilty soul. Is it hard to conjure up that picture? The God-man, looking His horrible death in the face, beginning already to be, as He Himself said, "sorrowful even unto death," would bolster up the fainting spirits of His friends before the dreadful ordeal begins. The last night on earth, He institutes the Blessed Sacrament, the greatest memorial of His love that even He could give. The face of the treasonous Apostle confronts Him amid His act of love, and as He looks deep into that hell-bound soul, can it be that He fails to call mentally at least to whatever of good there may be left in Judas? It is in vain. Christ·grows more plain and specific. He tells aloud of the treason of one of the company, and immediately, the Twelve reveal themselves in one of those unpremeditated, spontaneous actions that tell character so perfectly. They are, of course, stricken with horror at the thought that one of their number could fall so low. But there is no one of them that looks to another in suspicion. They ask, not "Who is it, Lord?" but rather, "Is it I, Lord?" Remarkable testimonial of their moral greatness! Each of them knows his weakness well enough to suspect himself before anyone else. Judas, compelled to ask the same question as the others to avoid arousing suspicion prematurely, hears the direct, damning answer: "Thou sayest it; that which thou doest, do quickly." Even then, Christ apparently did not expose Judas publicly to the others; St. John says they thought Christ's mysterious words had some connection with Judas's business capacity in regard to the festival day, or perhaps some instructions about an alms to the poor. But Judas knew well enough what Christ meant, and he obeys the command literally. He goes out to consummate his villainy, and quickly. One more chance spurned, one more opportunity to retrace his steps flung from him, he rushes through the gathering twilight to direct his mob to the Mount of Olives.

The climax of his hypocrisy is reached in the hideous irony of his kiss of betrayal. It is not enough for his low soul to sell his Lord; he must sound the depths of degradation and hypocrisy by betraying Him with the mark of friendship. It is the last word in villainy, certainly. But Christ's great heart is still not full to overflowing with hatred of His betrayer. Judas greets Him with the sign of friendship, hypocritical as it is. He returns the salutation with genuine friendship. Even in that terrible instance, when Judas reaches the lowest pit of sin, even then Christ calls him friend. It is the supreme moment, the greatest opportunity and the last. Christ will not have it said even of Judas that he fell because he had no chance to rise. The Saviour gives him that last chance to repent of his villainy, calls him friend in the midst of it, offers him then and there the forgiveness of a great-souled friend. But Judas is past that now. His kiss is delivered, his Victim is bound and dragged off, and the last act of the stupendous drama of man's Redemption is well begun.

The Apostles are scattered after Peter's impulsive attack on Malchus. Christ, surrounded by His enemies, is hauled from one court to another. Peter and then John follow Him from afar off into the very court of His judge; and Judas? Judas gets one glimpse of his own soul as it is in reality, and even he is frantic with horror. He would undo his foul work of treason, flings from him in horror the thirty silvery tokens of his degradation, is spurned by even his accomplices in crime with the contempt the traitor always merits, and completes his tale of lost opportunity by suicide. That is truly the end, the last opportunity. His guilt was enormous before, heaped up beyond all human calculation; he makes it worse now. The Christ who had called him friend would have been glad to act as friend had Judas made it possible. Peter sinned too, and so did the rest of the Twelve; all of them were faithless when the hour of test came. All of them repented, Judas included, repented bitterly, but with what a difference! The Eleven trusted Christ's love; Judas did not. The Eleven were Christ's heroes and martyrs afterward; Judas lives only in his treachery, the contempt and hatred of mankind. His last opportunity was gone, missed like all the others. Time and again in his apostolic career, Christ had offered him chances of better things; Judas missed them all. That note of lost opportunity is the keynote of his whole career; he was constantly spurning chances to rise above himself and his selfish degradation. The last of them he spurns as he had spurned the rest; he lives in memory as the greatest and most ignoble failure in the history of mankind.

12

PAUL, A Man's Man

TO COMPRESS St. Paul into a formula is hopeless. It is hard to state the essential character of any man, even the simplest, in a formulary. St. Paul is one of the most complex characters that ever lived, and to state his essential nature in a form of words is worse than useless to attempt. There is no more complex character than his in the Apostolic College. Those Thirteen range through all possible gradations of complexity from the simplicity of an Andrew or a Philip to the varied complexity of Paul; they are veritably all sorts and conditions of men, and at the zenith, so far as complexity of character and mingled qualities are concerned, stands the man who called himself the last and least of the Apostles, the great Apostle of the Gentiles. He was an effective preacher, none ever more so; his spoken words, reported, imperfectly of course, as they have been across the years, still have power to move and thrill, and there can be no greater test of power in the spoken word than that. As an orator, he has seldom, if ever, been surpassed in any age or nation. His address to the citizens of Athens, whom he found worshiping at an altar to the Unknown God is still a splendid example of powerful and effective oratory. He was a theologian who deserves to rank, on purely human grounds, be it noted, with theological intellects like Thomas of Aquin and Augustine. As an organizer and inspirer of often quite timid new Christian bodies he was unequaled. It is only a Francis Xavier who deserves to be ranked with him as a missionary, as a preacher of Christ Crucified to the pagan, and it was unquestionably Paul who inspired Francis in his noble efforts to spread the rule of Christ the King in men's hearts. As a writer, he is one of the world's greatest. The number is small of those who have been able so to spread their minds and souls on paper as to move and instruct and inspire not only those directly addressed, but generations and nations centuries away from the writer. That Paul was of that number, the Epistles demonstrate, for they still retain, almost two thousand years from Paul's day, their freshness, their power to stir and inspire, their sublime elevation. They are great literature, as well as inspired literature, and still they reflect but a scanty picture of their author. He was a great mystic, too, one of the greatest and most favored in Christian times, so that he could say of some of his experiences in the spiritual order: "Whether in the body or out of the body, I know not." Finally, he was able to say of himself, and he said it exultantly, joyfully: "I live, now not I, but Christ liveth in me." A great, many-sided man of genius, unquestionably, was Paul, but in being so, he did not cease to be a

thoroughly human man, a manly man in whom the
suspicion of anything effeminate or soft were ridicu-
lous. The manliness of his character is conspicuous,
unmistakable.

Take him at the period of his greatest activity, the
time when he was being conveyed to Rome a prisoner.
He was then about sixty years of age, vigorous, active,
forceful, manly, athletic. He was worn with years of
hardship and travel and labor, for he was no weakling
in any sense of the term. A lifetime of labor he had
already spent by that time, as men count lifetimes, and
the years had left their mark. He had felt the lash, as
we know from his own statement, no fewer than eight
times, and a Roman scourging was no joke. He had
been stoned once. Shipwreck had threatened his life
and worn his bodily powers three times. On one occasion, he spent a whole day and a night in an open
boat, at the mercy of the wind and waves in momen-
tary peril of his life. He had had painful experience
of Roman prisons, and they were no models of luxurious accommodation. Toil, hunger, thirst, labor,
danger, flight, penance, remorse — all these he had
known, and not merely in passing. They had made up
his life for thirty years. It is no matter for wonder if
we find him grizzled and worn and gray by the time
his sixth decade closed.

He had the features of the Jew, with something of
the refinement of the Greek about them. He was short
of stature, with a gray beard, and bald of head above a
high forehead. His eyes were gray, it would seem, and

bright originally, before he became what he himself calls "blear-eyed" — an expression that would seem to indicate some sort of ophthalmia. He combined the facial and cranial characteristics of the thinker and the man of action, and there was a set of determination to his jaw and chin that spoke his essential firmness and courage. The force of his will directed the power of a mind seldom equaled among men in power and brilliancy, so that when he appeared on the scene of action — and it usually became a scene of action when Paul appeared, no matter what it may have been before — men took notice and listened and usually obeyed, and that despite the handicap of what must have been a rather insignificant physique. It was insignificant in appearance, and only so; in endurance, it was the physique of an athlete. It had to be so to enable Paul to withstand the strenuous and painful life of labor and hardship that was his from earliest manhood.

From the intellectual standpoint, he was a giant. He was the only one of Christ's company of friends who had the equivalent of a college or university education. He had been trained in the best schools of the period. Hebrew he knew from birth, and Greek as well, probably. Some Latin may have come within the scope of his attainments, for there were men of his vicinity who knew Latin, and he seems to have been as avid for knowledge in his young manhood as he was for souls in later days. The vigor of his expression and the power of his language and style in oratory or in writing mark him as a man of superior intellectual attainments, and

be it remembered that he dictated his Epistles to secre-
taries and his speeches have come down to us through
the medium of shorthand report! In mental equip-
ment, therefore, and in mental achievement, too, he is
one of the world's great men. He is more; he is
one of the world's best-loved men, and in that fact, he
exhibits a difference from others of the world's greatest.
He does not merely excite a modern man's admiration;
Aristotle and Alexander and Cicero may do that, to a
degree. He arouses modern souls to love him for himself, and that argues qualities of soul that are unusual.
Barnabas and Titus loved him dearly; they have
modern company.

As in any other manly man's character, Paul's independent spirit was uppermost. Not the least prominent
feature of his physical make-up was the horny, calloused hand of the man. He was not above earning
his living with his hands. It was a thing of principle
for every Jew, of any and every station, to have some
manual trade at his beck and call. Paul was a tent-
maker, or better, probably, a maker of mohair from
which tents were made. He supported himself by his
trade, even when engaged in the greater trade of
preaching the Gospel of Christ. He did not permit the
faithful to support him, as did the other Apostles,
though he had as great a claim, the same claim, to that
support as had they. He, the genius, the scholar, the
preacher, the priest, supported himself by the labor of
his hands. And he tells his readers again and again
that he did so, not out of any spirit of false pride, but

in order not to be burdensome to the community. Once
he said to them: "I coveted no man's gold or silver or
apparel; ye yourselves know that these hands minis-
tered unto my necessities and to them that were with
me." Again: "We bear all things that we may cause
no hindrance to the Gospel of Christ. It were good for
me to die rather than that any man should make my
glorying vain." He would prefer even death, you see,
to dependence upon anyone so long as he could support
himself with the labor of his own hands while his
head and heart were engaged in the work of the ministry. He would not tolerate even the appearance of
dependence. That is the significance of that hardened
hand, not only that his enemies might have no pretext
for slander — and no man ever had more or bitterer
enemies — but also that his converts, whom he loved
with a love as tender as a mother's and as strong as a
father's, should have no reason to suspect him of self-
seeking. The Apostle would be above reproach in these
things that pertained to his manly spirit of
independence.

The basis of that spirit of independence was his
pride, honest, honorable pride. Not that he cared a fig
for position or repute, except insofar as it helped him
in his mission of spreading the Gospel of Christ in
men's minds. But proud he was, honorably proud, as
the veteran soldier is proud of his record, his cam-
paigns, his hard-won medals for valor, his victories, his
captain. In that spirit it was that Paul thrilled with
pride. He gloried, for instance, in his likeness through

suffering and humiliation to his Captain and Lord: "I bear branded on my body the marks of Jesus." He gloried in his position as one of the chosen instruments of the Gospel; he was joyously and mightily proud of his position as an Apostle of Christ. He begins most of his letters with the assertion of his Apostleship; "I, Paul, Apostle of Jesus Christ." He goes so far upon one occasion as to point out, with vigorous emphasis, that though he is the least of the Apostles, Apostle he is none the less, and as such, not one whit inferior to the others who entered the vineyard of the Lord while he was still a persecutor or even ignorant of the very existence of the Messias that had been foretold by the generations of prophets raised by God in the midst of His people. He is a genuine model of patriotic spirit and feeling, too. It is a proud boast of his, made on more than one occasion, that he was a Roman citizen. His ancestry was a matter of pride with him as well. A more ardent Jew never lived, though he came in time to recognize that the day of the Jewish religion and the Jewish nation was over forever because of their rejection of the Messias. He says, for example, on one occasion: "Are they Hebrews? So am I; are they Israelites? So am I. Are they the seed of Abraham? So am I, and yet more." He could boast of his descent from the generation of Abraham, but he could not at the same time fail to recognize that he had now, by the virtue of Christ's call to the apostolate, something more glorious of which to boast. He was proud, then, proud as every self-respecting man must be, proud of his dignities as one of the Apostles of Christ, proud of his citizenship in the greatest empire of ancient times, proud of his descent from Abraham's honored blood. But he was too great a man, too noble, to have even a speck of ignoble pride. His pride was based on an accurate self-knowledge and appreciation of himself. The same self-knowledge could not but make him humble.

He confessed that humility time and time again; there was not a trace or tinge of vanity or conceit about him. It is he himself who tells us of his shortcomings, both before he became an Apostle and afterward. Again and again, he alludes to the days when he persecuted the Church of Christ out of his mistaken zeal and hatred for things Christian. He was converted to Christ instantaneously and miraculously, but immediately after his conversion, he took himself to the desert to do penance and to prepare his great soul for the mission that divine guidance opened before him. He recounts the appearance of the Risen Christ to the Apostles and adds: "And finally, He appeared also to me, the least of the Apostles, as to one born out of due time." The least of the Apostles he counted himself, and it never entered into the man's great soul to vaunt his position as due to his own merits in any sense. It is always with a deep sense of his own unworthiness that he mentions his call to the apostolic dignity, and attributes it to the great mercy and benevolence of his Master. He humbles himself to the dust, more than once, in his Epistles. It is he, for instance, who tells us that he was afflicted with a permanent illness of some sort that made him an object of repugnance to those about him. And even spiritually, he was not above telling his readers for all time, he was afflicted, and grievously. He mentions that he was afflicted with a sting of the flesh, an angel of Satan to buffet him, a carnal temptation, it would appear. And he records the answer he received to his request to God for relief. It is not liberation from the temptation, from the buffetings of that angel of Satan, that he receives. He is told: "My grace is sufficient for you." A great soul he was, unquestionably; it is only a great spirit that can be so humble as to record his own deficiencies and failures. Littler men hide them; spiritual giants tell them, and in the telling, delineate their greatness.

So great a man as Paul could not fail to be a brave man, and from the viewpoint of character, there is nothing more conspicuous than Paul's bravery, physical and moral. Bodily perils, the hatred of old friends and their persecutions, charges of folly, accusations of treason to religion and nationality, misunderstanding, ingratitude, treachery — all of them Paul had to endure, and at the end of such a lifetime, the headman's ax. In the face of danger, he was a rock of courage. In the storm and shipwreck that befell him as he was taken prisoner to Rome to appear before Caesar, to whose judgment he had carried his appeal, it was Paul who stood firm amid the general panic and consternation. A great picture is that, of the little Apostle, a Jewish prisoner, taking command of the storm-driven ship and its fear-maddened company. It was a triumph of personality, and in that hour of danger, men recognized a man and obeyed, to their advantage, for not one life was lost. A great soul spoke and acted in an emergency, and littler men had perforce to listen and heed. But greater still than his physical courage was his moral bravery, the courage that impels a man to undertake disagreeable and dangerous enterprises for an ideal, the courage that drives a man to his duty in the face of any and every obstacle that seeks to hinder. It required a noble brand of spiritual courage for Paul to become a Christian after having been a persecutor of Christians. He had perforce to be a brave man morally to return after an absence of a few years to preach Christ and Him crucified to the people who had commissioned him and spurred him on in his efforts to exterminate the very memory of that self-same Christ. But back he went, boldly, armed only in his consciousness that he was right and that he spoke in the name of Christ. That word "boldly" turns up again and again in any account of Paul's spirit. Both he himself and Luke, in the Acts of Apostles, use the word repeatedly. It is expressive of Paul's outstanding characteristic. He was bold and straightforward and hewed to the line of duty; the chips might well be left to care for themselves. He withstood Peter boldly to his face, because he thought his chief mistaken in a point of policy. When brought before the Roman governor who had his life in his hands, Paul denounced him in open court. He aroused the ire of a Jewish mob, was rescued by the Roman guards and conducted to their barracks, and at once turned in the doorway and addressed that infuriated crowd. He stretched his hand above their heads in commanding gesture, and once more, a mob recognized its master and listened in awed silence to his message. The spell was soon broken and the mob became more infuriated than ever, and remember, it was the same mob that had stoned Stephen some time before for telling them of Christ. Even the captain of the guards was frightened and took Paul inside the castle; the only cool man in the scene was the storm-center of it. Paul faced the mob as he had faced mobs before, just as calmly as he faced his judge and was to bend his great head beneath the ax of the executioner. For his soul was unshakable; it was founded on the rock that is Christ. He had said: "I live, now not I, but Christ liveth in me." "He was a man, take him all in all, we shall not look upon his like again."

Name	Feast in Latin Rite	Symbol	Scene of Apostolic Labors	Death
Peter	June 29	One or two keys	Preached in Jerusalem; Bishop of Antioch; Pope and Bishop of Rome.	Crucified by order of Nero, 67 A.D.
Andrew	Nov. 30	X-shaped cross	Scythia, Greece, Constantinople.	Crucified on X-shaped cross at Patras in Achaia.
James, Greater ...	July 25	Staff, wallet	Jerusalem.	Beheaded by order of Herod Agrippa in Jerusalem; first Apostle martyred.
John	Dec. 27	Eagle, chalice	Asia Minor, Ephesus, Patmos; Guardian of Mary after death of Jesus.	Escaped martyrdom of boiling oil under Domitian; died at Ephesus.
Philip	May 1	Double cross	Phrygia, Asia Minor.	Crucified at Hieropolis.
Bartholomew	Aug. 24	Knife; or shown holding his own skin in his hand	Arabia, Parthia, India, Armenia.	Skinned alive in Armenia; crucified.
Thomas	Dec. 21	Spear, arrow	India, Far East.	Martyred at Meliabor, in India.

		Fuller's club	Bishop of Jerusalem.	Stoned to death in Jerusalem.
James, Less	May 1		Bishop of Jerusalem.	Stoned to death in Jerusalem.
Matthew	Sept. 21	Short sword, winged man bearing lance	Arabia, Egypt.	Martyred at Nodabar in Parthia.
Thaddeus Jude ..	Oct. 28	Club	Syria, Mesopotamia, Persia.	Tied to a cross and shot to death with arrows in Armenia.
Simon Zelotes	Oct. 28	Saw	North Africa, Persia.	Crucified in Persia by idolatrous priests.
Judas Iscariot	....	....	....	Hung himself, after betraying Jesus for 30 pieces of silver.
Matthias	Feb. 24	Lance	Chosen by Apostles to replace Judas; details of life not known.	Stoned and beheaded in Colchis.
Paul	June 29	Sword	As "Apostle of Gentiles," made three missionary journeys to Mediterranean countries.	Beheaded at Rome, 67 A.D.